ABIDE

A Story of Grief and Faith
Written for the grieving soul

JAMIE MARIE OGIAMIEN (LAMPERT)

ISBN 979-8-89112-768-5 (Paperback)
ISBN 979-8-89112-769-2 (Digital)

Copyright © 2024 Jamie Marie Ogiamien (Lampert)
All rights reserved
First Edition

All rights reserved. No part of this publication may be reproduced, distributed, or transmitted in any form or by any means, including photocopying, recording, or other electronic or mechanical methods without the prior written permission of the publisher. For permission requests, solicit the publisher via the address below.

Covenant Books
11661 Hwy 707
Murrells Inlet, SC 29576
www.covenantbooks.com

To "abide is a verb. It is active. Abiding in Christ is not a feeling or a belief but something we do. It means to 'remain' or 'stay' and entails far more than the idea of continued belief in the savior" ("Three Keys to Abide in Christ" by Erik Reed [under subtitle "Jesus Invites You to Abide"]. Erik Reed, "Three Keys to Abide in Christ," Open the Bible with Pastor Colin Smith [April 24, 2017] [openthebible.org]. Abide in me, and I in you.) (John 15:4–5).

To Seth David-Owen Lampert.
Grief is the cost of love.

Contents

Introduction ix

1. Anticipated Grace 1
2. Surrounded 11
3. We Cannot Put God in a Box 19
4. Personal Touch 28
5. Dreams: Everything Will Be Okay 34
6. Patient and Kind 39
7. Love Not of This World 45
8. Made in His Image 54
9. Beauty from Ashes 60
10. Eternal Hope 68

Life after Loss 77
Stories of Seth from the Mouths of Others: Seth as a Person 101
Letter in Honor of My Brother 117
References 131

Introduction

I am writing this book in honor of my baby brother Seth David-Owen Lampert. He passed away unexpectedly in 2019 shortly after his twenty-sixth birthday. He and I were extremely close. I loved him more than words can express, and I know he felt the same. We would do anything for each other. Before I felt complete peace that he is doing well now, I used to beg God to take me instead of him. Thanks to God's daily and gentle care, I now have complete peace that he is not only doing okay but thriving! I know Seth is surrounded by perfect peace and love, without need or hurt. This does not take away how much I miss him or how I long for a Seth hug or laugh. I still live with daily "I wish" moments or "what if" moments, imagining Seth in my day-to-day now—him playing with my youngest daughter who didn't get to see, be held by, or meet him; him being the best uncle to his niece Olivia. I know he would have made every soccer game, every dance recital, anything, and everything important to his nieces. He loved being an uncle and adored her! A friend told me the other day that they saw Seth just days before his accident. I was three months pregnant with my second daughter and very sick with my second round of hyperemesis gravidarum (HG). HG left me bedridden, feeding off a central line. My friend saw him and said, "I can't believe Jamie is going through this all over again, especially knowing how sick she gets."

Seth's response was "I know, but Olivia is perfect. All you have to do is meet her, and it makes it all worth it." He loved her *big*! Still does. Somehow, someway I know he has met his youngest niece Brooklyn, and I know he is equally obsessed with her. While I have been angry at myself over mine and my brother's last few interactions, I found a note that he wrote to me for my twenty-eighth birthday that said, "You were a 'perfect child,' great sister, and probably the second-best mom I know. Anyone is lucky to have you as family or a friend. Don't be too hard on yourself. You're the best person I know. Love, your little brother Seth Lampert." So, I am trying to listen to him.

Grief is complex. It is rarely, if ever, a single emotion. I've learned I can be sad, angry, happy, in celebration, frustrated, the list goes on—sometimes all at once. This book starts with me in a pit of despair. Physically hurting from grief. Unable to cope or function from my grief. Looking back, I see how I was surrounded. I see how God was caring for us, even Seth, in the small and big details of our tragedy. And as my grief has changed over time, I can see the fingerprints of God over all areas of healing. I am so in awe of how God meets us where we're at and tends to us so intimately, refusing to leave us in that "pit." His love is targeted and detailed. My eyes have been opened to God's love for Seth, myself, and all of his children. I have been forever changed by the loss of my brother. He took a part of me with him the day he left this side of heaven, but I have seen the sweet mercy of Jesus help us through this tragedy. So much so that I don't look at my Savior the same. Many attributes are the same, but my understanding of his love/mercy is much richer. The way he knows exactly what we are feeling, and how to meet us in our needs is inconceivable to me. This book shares a little of my mine and my brother's story. It talks about my grief, but most importantly, it talks about an all-knowing, all-caring, and able God who meets us in our "pits" or despair and carries us till we can stand on two feet again. A God who abides in us so we can follow his lead and abide in him. What a gift to be so entangled by his love/grace that it forever changes our perspective of him.

Seth, this book was written in honor and in dedication to your loving and generous spirit. You were the kindest, funniest, most talented, and brightest soul. May we all love without bias or judgment like you. May we all have open arms, tables, and homes to the person hurting or in need like you. I hope our story can help others who experience deep loss. As always, help me to love well.

Love you, Seth David-Owen Lampert.

Your "Sissy,"
Jamie Marie Ogiamien (Lampert)
xoxo

1

Anticipated Grace

Before they call, I will answer, while they are yet speaking, I will hear. (Isaiah 65:24)

Your Father knows what you need before you ask Him. (Matthew 6:8)

Many of the Samaritans from the town believed in him because of the woman's testimony. He told me everything I ever did. So, when the Samaritans came to him, they urged him to stay with them and he stayed two days. And all because of his words many more became believers. (John 4:39–41)

And he said, O Lord, God of my master Abraham, please grant me success today and show steadfast love to my master Abraham…Before he had finished speaking, behold Rebekah…the man bowed his head and worshiped the Lord. (Genesis 24:11–28)

In 2013, my younger brother had a near-death experience (NDE). He told me about it a couple months later. He came to visit me in

Southern California at my college to help me move; my graduation from nursing school at Biola University was just around the corner. It was not unheard of for Seth and me to have conversations about faith. My belief in Christ was well known to our family, friends, and members of our small town. Seth had a more complex or less obvious relationship with the Lord, for lack of a better description. I do not doubt he believed, but his transformation journey took a very unique path. He was known for that, not being a follower but setting his own pace. I admired that about him. Although, as a protective older sister, it could be frustrating at times to watch him learn the hard or long way.

I have a somewhat vivid memory, very vivid memory compared to other memories from that time, of Seth and I as kids in our upstairs "playroom." He was around seven to eight years old, and I was around nine to ten years old. He and his friend had lightheartedly teased me earlier that day about the Bible verses covering my bedroom door. I guess he felt bad for teasing me because he apologized. He went on to tell me how he admired that I never backed down from my faith even when it was an unpopular thing. Then he said he wanted to have God in his life as well and asked me to pray for him. We prayed together and asked Jesus into his life. I was a new Christian myself. I gave myself to the Lord at camp as an eight-year-old, so I am sure the prayer was simple. But I know it was sincere because I remember the moment and the tenderness of it. Seth and I were a lot alike. I've recently reflected on this. We both empathized deeply with others, which unfortunately means we both tend to take on the pain of others. When I do this, I turn mostly, not all the time, to my faith and my church for relief. I cope with prayer, music, journaling, reading, and verbal processing with like-minded friends or counselors. From what I can tell, as an observer of Seth, he tried to fix everyone's problems by taking them on himself. He often used comedy as a coping mechanism, distraction, and sometimes substances to numb the pain.

In 2013, his NDE was related to an unintentional overdose. He told me this in my Biola house the weekend he came to visit. From what he told me, he was unconscious for at least twelve hours.

His friends had taken him to the ER; they were worried and frantic, who are still great friends to this day. During the time Seth was unconscious, he had an out-of-this-world experience. He went on to describe through his tears, "Jamie, I have never felt so at peace and loved. I can't explain it. I was completely peaceful and the light and love that surrounded me was so real and unexplainable." He went on to say that after being loved to his core, surrounded by light and peace. He then began to visit everyone he knew. He felt as though he was saying goodbye. Each visit felt like seconds and hours at the same time. There was no sense of time. He said, "Life seems dull now. I just want to be surrounded by that light, love, and peace again. I have never felt so loved or accepted."

He went on to describe the small and big details. He said, "Everything was so much more real and alive. I could see miles away the fine details of things without straining or trying." He mentioned traveling with a thought. Sitting at the dinner table, exchanging laughs and goodbyes with loved ones. He said he saw everyone; not a single person that he loved was missed, but he pointed out his dinner at his best friend Vinnie's childhood home with Vinnie's whole family. He said, "I felt so alive. Everything feels like a dream now, like I am living in black and white. I feel the wind, but it doesn't feel real." He didn't really feel "alive" anymore but like things were just passing him by. He told me, "Jamie, I cannot deny God. I know he is real. But I feel so stuck, it's empty here."

I was crying with him, and I said, "Seth, that overwhelming love and peace you experienced is how God feels about you every moment of every day no matter if it's a good or bad day." We talked and cried until we went to sleep.

The next morning, I took him to my church, Vineyard Anaheim. Pastor Lance talked about how God's character is multifaceted like a diamond. I didn't know it at the time, but afterward, Seth told me about his infatuation with diamonds. He was wearing an ace of diamond necklace that day; he held it and cried throughout the service. He told me after the service that he felt like Pastor Lance wrote the message just for him and how it felt like they were the only two people in the room. At the end of the message, we did small group gatherings for communion. It was a pretty big church, so we gathered up with the people sitting around us. Our group included a few people I recognized, but no one I knew well (besides my boyfriend at the time who's now my husband). A few of the group members I had never seen before. We took turns praying as a group over communion and each other. When Seth prayed, he continued to cry. I remember a part of his prayer that made me cry; he thanked God for all the prayers I had prayed for him throughout his life. He mentioned something like "I had no idea how often she prayed for me until now."

A man I've never met came up to him to pray. He said, "I feel like recently your world was turned upside down, like you were going full speed in one direction, and you hit a wall. I know how that can be, it happened to me. It stopped you in your tracks and now you must choose. You can't have both. It's the world or God." Then he prayed encouragement and words of truth/worth over Seth. Another woman came up to Seth and said, "The Lord told me to tell you you're here for a reason. God's not done with you yet. There's still more he has for you, it's not an accident you're here." Then she prayed encouragement and truth over his life. The first man to pray for him pointed to his necklace and said, "Look, ace of diamonds, just like God showed us in Bible study last week" to the man standing next to him. Then that man also began to pray over Seth specific words of encouragement and prophecies. Seth's tears were heavy, but they were not sad. They were tears of relief; he felt loved and seen.

As we drove home again, he said, "Jamie, I cannot deny God, but how do we know we can trust the Bible if it's written by imperfect people?" At the time, I did not have an answer for him, and I'm glad because I think my answer would be different today; I mostly just listened. Later that day, we went to the Sunday evening service at my church. A man named Jerry, who I'd never met before, came up to Seth during the meet and greet to say hi. He asked Seth what his name was. When he responded, "Seth," Jerry said, "Aw, like Seth in the Bible."

Seth responded, "I don't really read the Bible."

Jerry said, "Aw, man, you're missing out. The Bible saved me. It's the word of life." He proceeded to write his name and number in his own Bible; he then handed it to Seth and said, "Take this, call or text with any questions. We can go through it together." Jerry asked if Seth would go forward to pray together; Seth did. I didn't hear their prayer, but they talked for a while after. Seth told me on the ride home that Jerry told him his story. He told Seth how he was saved on an ICU bed after surviving multiple stab wounds. He told Seth how he "heard" every prayer ever prayed for him while unconscious on that ICU bed, including the many prayers by his grandma. When we got in the car, Seth was emotional again and he said, "Jamie, I can't deny God. I heard every prayer you ever prayed for me too, thank you." He started reading Jerry's Bible, and I know they sent texts. That was the last time I saw Jerry, and I am unsure of how long they continued to talk.

This special weekend of deep talks with my brother was life-altering and faith-increasing for both Seth and me. I believe God anticipated what we needed. He knew Seth felt stuck and alone. He knew he needed encouragement and faith-building prophesies. He knew he needed a personal touch, and without Seth even knowing exactly what to ask for, God answered. He knew his spoken and unspoken needs more intimately than Seth knew himself. He sent the right people with the right heart and words. He prepared them for Seth earlier in the week at Bible study. He gave Pastor Lance the sermon to speak that Sunday. He brought Jerry and Seth together, knowing the similarities of their stories and Seth's questions about the Bible. Not only did it immensely increase my faith and understanding of God's ability to intimately care for our needs in the moment. But God anticipated my need for reassurance *years* later.

In February 2019, my little brother Seth was in a car accident, which took his life. I remember getting the news; my whole body gave out. I just remember screaming at the top of my lungs, "No NOOOOOOO NOO!" over and over. It was between 4:00 and 5:00 a.m. I had been up with a stomachache since midnight, which was weird. I was three months pregnant at the time enduring my second round of HG. I had not eaten solid food in weeks. I was getting all my hydration and nutrients through my PICC line (peripherally inserted central catheter). I received continuous TPN (total parenteral nutrition) and daily banana bags (a form of IV hydration/electrolyte replacement). I could not walk without violently throwing up, and sometimes I even lost my balance or fell due to electrolyte imbalance or muscle weakness/atrophy as a result of being bedridden. I often threw up streaks of blood from ruptured blood vessels in my esophagus. I had burning "stuff" come out of my eyes when I threw up violently, and I would dream of drinking water or lemonade because I was so thirsty and dehydrated. So to be up with an upset stomach not involving nausea or vomiting was abnormal at the time. My upset stomach started around midnight, which I later learned was around the time of his accident.

I was finally able to go back to bed and had some relief between 4:00 and 5:00 a.m. Now I know his time of death was at 4:19 a.m. on February 5. My body was somehow reacting to the grief before I heard any news of his accident or passing. (I later found out my aunt Christy was up the same length of time with similar symptoms before receiving the news. She and our uncle Chris met my parents at the hospital, so my parents weren't alone and my aunt and uncle could say goodbye to Seth with them.) Once I finally went back to bed, my two-year-old daughter lay sleeping next to me. My phone rang, but I ignored it since I'd been up all night with the stomachache. Then my husband's phone rang, and I said, "Answer it, it might be about Seth or Amanda," sensing it might be urgent being the second call so early in the morning. I always worried about Seth and a best friend of mine had just received a double lung transplant only a month earlier, so I worried it could be concerning her as well. My husband answered; I shot up in bed when I heard my mom tell my husband the news through the phone.

All I could do was scream, "No, NOOOOOOO, NOOOO NOOO! IT'S NOT POSSIBLE. SETH. NOOOOOOO, MY BABY BROTHER, NOOOOOO!" over and over. Thankfully, by the grace of God, my daughter slept soundly. My husband was in shock. He kept saying, "This isn't real. It can't be." My mom said her best friend Ronda, who is like a second mom to me, was on the way to my house to watch Olivia so

I could come say goodbye before the coroner came to take him. Unfortunately, as Ronda arrived, my mom called back to tell me the coroner had already arrived to take Seth's body from the hospital. I was devastated. I didn't get to say goodbye. To hug him one more time. Pray for him one more time. Hold his hand one more time. Kiss his cheek one more time. My parents didn't call earlier because I was so sick. My aunt Christy later told me I might have had a hard time having the image of Seth on that hospital bed as my last image of him. Even though it hurts that I didn't get to say goodbye in person, I am sure God had a reason behind it. I sat in my bed with my daughter sleeping next to me. My husband sitting in shock. Ronda hugged me and stroked my hair as I screamed and cried for hours. I didn't know my body could hold so many tears, my comforter was soaking wet on my lap. My parents stopped by on their way home from the hospital to check on us. I asked a few questions because I was worried for my brother and wanted to know he was okay in his last moments. But I think I held a lot in while trying to be strong for my parents. I know they did the same trying to be strong for me. I spent the next several weeks, unable to sleep. My eyes swollen almost shut from crying and sleep deprivation. I would lay awake all day and all night, wondering if my brother was okay the night of the accident and in all the moments to follow. Did he feel pain? Was he alone? Did he know how much I loved him? Is he with God? Is he in heaven? I didn't get to say goodbye. He didn't get to meet Brooklyn. As millions of questions and "what ifs" ran through my head, God reminded me often of the things Seth told me about his NDE in 2013. I would ask the question…and God would remind me. "I felt the most loved and at peace I have ever felt. I was saying goodbye to everyone I loved. I heard every prayer you ever prayed for me. I was surrounded by a warm peaceful light." Specific answers to all my questions directly from Seth's mouth, spoken five years prior. Looking back, I sometimes feel God allowed Seth to experience his NDE in 2013 for me, just as much if not more, than he allowed it for him. He anticipated my need and, in his infinite mercy, allowed me to hear the answers to my desperate questions directly from my brother himself after experiencing a detailed NDE. Sometimes my prayers were just screams, moans, and sobs; but God knew what I needed years before I was desperate for answers and reassurance. His anticipated grace met me where I was. He abided in me, so I could follow his lead and abide in him. But it doesn't stop there. On top of God's personalized gift of mercy, he continued to reassure me daily with gifts and miracles in order to assure and reassure my broken heart.

Sidenote: God often speaks to me through music and lyrics. A group called Mavrick City Music was established in 2018, and I discovered them in 2019 when my grief was all-consuming. Not to mention, shortly after my brother passed away, COVID hit. A pandemic can be isolating and lonely on a normal day, but especially while deeply grieving. God used music to help me feel less alone. I felt understood. Some of the lyrics spoke directly to my soul. They have been a gift to my grieving heart as well as the lyrics of many other Christian artist that I love. I have decided to add full or partial lyrics to songs that helped me through the toughest time of my life at the end of every chapter. I hope their lyrics bring peace to other souls like they have and continue to bring peace to mine. I encourage you to look them up and enjoy the full gift that they are.

Below is a link to the songs for your convenience. (https://youtube.com/playlist?list=PLT695EH94SC-hiM1sB-GOb0edyP5agRdJn&si=JCWgOzsaItpz5oRr)

Million Little Miracles
Elevation Worship and Maverick City Music

All my life I've been carried by grace
Don't ask me how cause I can't explain
It's nothing short of a miracle I'm here
I've got some blessings that I don't deserve
I've got some scares but that's how you learn
I think it over and it doesn't add up
I know it comes from above
I've got miracles on miracles a million little miracles
Count your miracles 1 2 3 4 I can't even count them all

ABIDE

You held me steady so I wouldn't give up
You opened doors that nobody could shut
I hope I never get over what you've done
I want to live with an open heart
I want to live like I know who you are
I hope I never get over what you've done
It's not coincidence and it's not luck
I know it comes from above
I've got miracles on miracles a million little miracles
I can't even count them all
I try and I can't keep up
Like when you healed my mother
You redeemed my father
Even in the death of my brother
you were closer than no other
You broke my chains
You saved my life
You set me free
You gave me victory
I've got miracles on miracles a million little miracles
I can't even count them all
You kept my mind right
You healed my body Jesus
I try and I can't keep up
Because every day there's a new miracle
I got breath in my lungs
I got clothes on my back
My mother would say
I got food on my table—Lord I know that you're able
Too many to count.

JAMIE MARIE OGIAMIEN (LAMPERT)

Give Me Faith
Acoustic Elevation Worship

I need you to soften my heart
And break me apart
I need you to open my eyes and see that you're shaping my life
All I am, I surrender
Give me faith to trust what you say
That you're good and your love is great
I'm broken inside, I give you my life
I need you to soften my heart to break me apart
I need you to pierce through the dark and cleanse every part of me
All I am I surrender
Give me faith to trust what you say, that
you're good and your love is great
I'm broken inside, I give you my life, it's yours
I may be weak but your spirits strong in me
My flesh may fail but my God you never will
I may be weak but your spirits strong in me
My flesh may fail, but my God you never will
Give me faith to trust what you say, that
you're good and your love is great
I'm broken inside, I give you my life
I may be weak but your spirits strong in me
My flesh may fail but my God you never will

2

Surrounded

He found him in a desert land, and in the wilderness; He encircled him, He cared for him, He guarded him as the pupil of His eye. (Deuteronomy 32:10)

You have enclosed me behind and before; And laid your hand upon me. (Psalm 139:5)

And I will be to her a wall of fire all around, declares the Lord. And I will be the glory in her midst. (Zechariah 2:5)

Be merciful unto me, O God, be merciful unto me: for my soul trusteth in thee; yea, in the shadow of thy wings will I make my refuge, until these calamities be overpast. (Psalm 57:1)

The lord is near to all who call on him, to all who call on him in truth. (Psalm 145:18)

The angel of the lord encamps around those who fear him, and he delivers them. (Psalm 34:7)

JAMIE MARIE OGIAMIEN (LAMPERT)

> You are my hiding place; you will protect me from trouble and surround me with songs of deliverance. (Psalm 32:7)

> As the mountains surround Jerusalem, so the lord surrounds his people both now and forevermore. (Psalm 125:2)

It was hard to see fully in the midst of tragedy, but I knew I was not alone then, and now I can see we were surrounded.

Ronda was there; she was holding me when I could not hold myself. A few hours later, I called five of my closest friends. They cried with me over the phone. They all loved Seth like family as well. They dropped what they were doing and came ASAP. I went to my parents' house, even though I had not been able to leave the house in weeks due to my HG and being bedridden because I could not be alone with my thoughts. Our house was full. Everyone left work on a Tuesday to surround us. Friends and family came from near and far.

As I worked up the courage to ask my parents more detailed questions of the night before, I learned how surrounded Seth was as well. He had just left a house with lifelong friends and our younger cousin. He was giving a young girl a ride home whom he had met that night. Apparently, the car slipped on black ice. He did not have his seat belt on. I cannot say for sure, but I speculate after hearing the details of his accident that my brother jumped in front of his passenger to protect her. It is without a doubt something my brother would do, even just meeting her that night. Had his seat belt been on and he was unable to protect her, I don't think he could have lived with himself. My gut tells me he died a hero, even though I'll never know for sure, maybe in heaven, I will know in full.

When she woke up, she found him lying on her lap. The car hit a tree on the passenger side, and Seth's left side of his head was bleeding where it hit the dashboard. She woke up, and after moving Seth off her lap, she ran for help. Limping and injured, she found a house and had them call 911. Even just meeting my brother that night, she cared so deeply and wanted to help him. When the firemen/ambulance arrived, they just so happened to be three young men and a fire chief, all long-time residents from our small community. Apparently, Seth was not recognizable due to his injuries, but they immediately knew it was him after cutting off his shirt and seeing his large wolf tattoo on his left ribcage. They were instructed to break protocol and call my parents seeing how bad of condition my brother was in.

My dad who is often away for weeks and even months for work during the winter months had just returned home from a work trip earlier that day. My parents got the call and were able to meet my brother at the hospital. I was told by the young men first to the scene that they had never seen our friend drive as fast as he did that night on the way to the hospital. They were all by Seth's side and cared so deeply for him. They told me the young woman who was in the accident with Seth refused to let him "go alone" in the ambulance, so she went with him as well for support. The idea of him in an ambulance alone with strangers killed me until I found out he had four people with him who cared so deeply for his well-being.

At the hospital, when Seth was out of surgery for the bleeding in his brain, my parents got to pray over him. According to my mom, he was never conscious and was breathing on a ventilator, but they prayed Psalm 23 over him, and as they finished, he breathed his last breath without the medical team touching the ventilator. If it wasn't for God allowing lifelong friends of ours to be on duty that night, friends that knew Seth's tattoo/cross necklace and friends who had my parents' numbers saved in their phones; my parents would not have known of Seth's accident or his passing until the next day. If my dad had not come home from his work trip, my mom would have been alone, and my dad would not have had the opportunity to be by his side and say goodbye. As hard as it was for them to be there that night, I can't thank God enough for allowing our mom and dad to be at his bedside, reciting Psalm 23 over him, as he went to be with Jesus. My mom even talks about how she felt held by Jesus walking down the hospital hall and in his room. It was the hardest night of all of our lives, but we cannot deny that we were surrounded.

The days and weeks to follow did not get any easier, but we continued to be surrounded. The calls, text messages, meals, and cards never seemed to stop. If you ever question reaching out to someone experiencing loss, do it; it means the world even if it's a simple "I love you." Sometimes, the simpler, the better. My aunt Soni, Uncle Hub, and cousins Casey, Alex, and Sofia jumped on the next flight home from their vacation. My aunt cooked for all the people at our house. Neighbors, friends, community members, and even people we didn't know well brought food, gifts, or kind words. I was too sick to shower independently for Seth's funeral due to my HG, so two of my mom's best friends Rita and Ronda taped up my PICC line and proceeded to give me a shower while I lay on the bathtub floor, throwing up. Ronda typed my speech that I wrote in bed for Seth's service. My cousins sat with me and talked about Seth while we hugged and cried together. Our church prayed for us and with us.

My husband's side of the family, which I was still getting to know called and left messages. My in-laws, also a newer relationship, flew in for Seth's service just to fly back the same day. I feel like that was the first time I felt loved by them; it meant so much to me. College friends sent flowers and cards. My coworkers sent flowers. My dad's coworker Heather made Seth's slide show for his service, and many of his colleagues came to Seth's service. I had friends driving from far to be there to support me. His service not only filled a large basketball gym (the one our parents, Seth, and I grew up playing in and I coach in now), but there was not enough room for everyone to come in. I was told some stood outside the door for the entire service. Friends of my parents and community members brought all the food and decorations. One close friend of my mom's even paid for the catered dinner tab at the restaurant, which was open invitation to all after the service.

The week after his service, I was still not sleeping; my concern for my brother had taken over. I always felt so protective of him, so responsible for his well-being and happiness. His death felt too final to bear, and I could not check on him. I did not know if he was okay, and I did not know how to protect him. It tormented me. Mine and my husband's dear friends and mentors showed up in their RV from Southern California to check on us and pray for us. They bought us dinner and planned to spend one night in front of our house in their

RV just to be with us. *I needed this!* I was so broken; I had so many questions and didn't know where to find answers to them. This was definitely the best gift I've ever received in my life. They just came; I didn't even have to ask. They're two of the wisest people I know, and I trust their discernment and words so deeply. I opened up and shared my concerns for Seth and his salvation. It was like word vomit; normally, I am more reserved, but I trust these two wholeheartedly, and I needed relief. I needed answers. I started from the beginning, our prayer as kids, Seth's life the good and bad, our miracle weekend, Seth's NDE (I didn't even know NDEs were a thing and relatively common until sharing with the Gillentines; they helped me make sense of this treasure of Seth's I'd know about but didn't understand the significance of for years).

They read Seth's poems, and we talked for hours. They let me process everything out loud; they listened intently, encouraged me, and prayed throughout. They were both so reassured and pointed out all the ways God's hand was on Seth's life. I'd feel relief then doubt would creep back in, so I'd ask the same questions. They would smile and continue to reassure me in the years to come I had a lot of moments like this with God. Gentle, kind reminders and reassurance even though my repetitive ways almost made God smile in amusement. Mr. Gillentine told me while not all Christians believe the same, he believed once saved, always saved. I believe this now, too, especially if someone is open to God but struggling. It's a matter of the heart, and only God knows the sincerity of each heart.

After all, I would make it as easy and straightforward as possible for my children to be able to spend eternity with me; a sincere desire would be all I need. They continued to read all of Seth's poems as I went to sleep that night and, the next morning, continued to reassure me. They said while Seth's writing shows a lot of hurt and struggle, God was also obvious in them. They asked if I had read the book *Evading Death's Grip* by Dr. Steven L. Long, which I had not. That's when he introduced the fact that there are books about NDEs, and Seth's experience has many similarities to stories he has read. Again, I knew people had NDEs, but I didn't know there were stories documented, and I had not realized what Seth told me in 2013 may have been an NDE. They prayed over us in the spirit multiple times. My mom came over that morning to be prayed over before they left. That unplanned visit meant the world to me. I needed someone I could trust to help me process, someone I felt safe with that demonstrated regularly relying on God for wisdom. Within a couple days of their visit, a book appeared on our doorstep from Amazon—*Evading Death's Grip* by Dr. Steven W. Long. I started it that night and did not put it down until it was done. Seth's NDE was holding me together, and this book validated everything he said. The book recommended other books on NDE, which began my healing journey. I read many books that year on heaven and NDEs including *Imagine Heaven* by John Burke; *To Heaven and Back* by Mary C. Neal, MD; *Proof of Heaven* by Eben Alexander, MD; *Life After Life* by Raymond A. Moody Jr., MD; *90 Minutes in Heaven* by Don Piper; *Physicians' Untold Stories* by Scott J. Kolbaba, MD; *Heaven* by Randy Alcorn; *Heaven is for Real* by Todd Burpo. Each time I finished one, I ordered another. They reassured me and confirmed not only what Seth told me but also how well he's doing now in heaven.

We were so surrounded. Tragedy stuck, and I do not want that for anyone. But God went before us, beside us, and behind us. He gathered the right people. He held us up when we were unable to hold ourselves.

Surrounded
Fight my Battles, Upperroom (YouTube)

There's a table that you prepared for me
In the presence of my enemies
It's your body and your blood you shed for me
This is how I fight my battles
And I believe you've overcome
And I will lift my soul in praise for what you've done
This is how I fight my battles
In the valley I know that you're with me
And surely your goodness and your mercy follow me
So, my weapons are praise and thanksgiving

ABIDE

This is how I fight my battles
And I believe you have overcome
And I will lift my soul in praise for what you've done
O Jesus
Calling on your name is how I fight
It may look like I am surrounded but I'm surrounded by you
I know the truth…when my enemies seem to be all around me
I know
I'm starting to see the darkness around me
is just the shadow of your wings
My victory's in Jesus' name
My victory's in that third day
My victory is in that third day
This is how I fight my battles
Praise
O thank you
Now my heart is bursting from the seams with praise inside of me
Praise will be my song
I will not contain this love.

"Another in the Fire"
Amanda Cook, Bethel Music YouTube

There's a grace when the heart is under fire
Another way when the walls are closing in
And I look at the space between
where I used to be and this reckoning
I know I will never be alone
There was another in the fire standing next to me
There's another in the water holding back the seas
And should I ever need reminding of how I've been set free
There is a cross that bears the burden where another died for me
There is another in the fire
All my debt left for dead beneath the waters
I'm no longer a slave to my sin anymore
And should I fall in the space between

JAMIE MARIE OGIAMIEN (LAMPERT)

What remains of me and this reckoning
Either way I won't bow to the things of this world
And I know I will never be alone
There is another in the fire standing next to me
There's another in the water holding back the seas
And should I ever need reminding what power set
me free there is a grave that holds no body
And now that power lives in me
I can see the light in the darkness as the darkness bows to him
I can hear the roar of the heavens as the space between wears thin
I can feel the ground shake beneath us as the prison walls cave in
Nothing stands between us
Nothing stands between us
There is no other name but the name that's Jesus
He who was and still is and will be through it all
So come what may in the space between all
the things unseen and this reckoning
I know I will never be alone
I know I will never be alone
There'll be another in the fire standing next to me
And should I ever need reminding of how good
you've been to me I'll count the joy come ev'ry
battle 'cause I know that's where you'll be.

3

We Cannot Put God in a Box

> Where were you when I laid the foundation of the earth? Tell me if you have understanding. (Job 38:4)
>
> All Power is given unto me in heaven and in Earth. (Matthew 28:18)
>
> He carried me away in the spirit to a great and high mountain, and showed me the Holy city, Jerusalem, coming down out of heaven from God. (Revelations 21:10)

God began to speak to me in big and little ways immediately after Seth's passing and continued to do so as I grieved. To be honest, I feel like the signs and wonders slowed down more recently as I have felt reassured and at peace with Seth's well-being. That, or I am less aware to receive them as I have gained some sense of normalcy again. I've heard the verse Psalm 34:18 many times throughout my life, but to experience it firsthand allows for a much deeper understanding of God's character. "The Lord is close to the brokenhearted and saves those who are crushed in spirt." How very true. He saved me, and when I see others hurting, I want to fix their problems, then I remember how close God was in my grief/depression. I don't have to fix anything for others, just be present and willing to be obedient with my time and resources. God does all the mending in the most beautiful, personal, and miraculous ways.

I love the clip in the 2019 movie about Mr. Rogers; he talks about death being human, mentionable and manageable, then he leans toward the man on his deathbed, a man with many regrets in life, and whispers something to him. When his friend/mentee, the son of the dying man, asked what he whispered to his father, he said, "I asked him to pray for me. I figure anyone going through what he's going through must be awfully close to God." He understood it; God is nearby always but intimately close to the brokenhearted or crushed in spirit. He knows what it is to suffer and to have deep loss. He knows our deepest needs and soul desires. He can meet us where we're at and save us, whatever that looks like for each individual. God did that for me constantly, and people questioned my experiences, which was painful because they were such gifts; but now I know better. Who are we to question a gift from God? Didn't he create the earth and heavens? Doesn't he have all power, and don't we have proof of his signs and wonders? We cannot put God in a box. He's too big for our finite minds to comprehend. While we're made in his image and he has given us many abilities, we're still so limited compared to his vastness. Thank you, Lord, for being near to my broken heart and mending it in the most perfect and patient ways.

A few days after my brother's accident, in February 2019, we were all at my parents' house. The house was full, as I mentioned in the previous chapter. I was missing him, staring at pictures in shock, trying to wrap my mind around the fact that I would not see him or experience him again physically. Then my mom's friend Nina saw something sticking out from under the coffee table. It was a small card from a gift bag, string still attached, that said, "To Olivia from Uncle Seth," in his handwriting. Nina handed it right to me. It was from Christmas a couple months before. I needed something physical from him. To see his handwriting, a personal note for Olivia came at the perfect time. To think all the times the house was cleaned from Christmas to February, and that day, in that moment, it stuck out just enough right when my heart was longing for a physical touch from him. It was a sign; it was a gift.

Around the same time, a friend of my mom's told me how God spoke to her the day of Seth's accident. She was driving home to Oregon from our small town of Cloverdale, and as she was driving, her phone rang with the news. Panic took over, so she called her brother Justin. She needed to be able to drive safely so her brother told her to focus on driving while he prayed for her. As he prayed for her, she said a semitruck swerved in front of her. Things seemed to move in slow motion in that moment, as if the world seemed to stop for a second. Her vehicle seemed to be on autopilot. On the back of the semitruck was a painted eagle that reminded her of Seth. My brother was obsessed with wolves; he called himself the "lone wolf." He also was known for his love of nature and native American culture passed on to us by our Grandpa Dave. Bobbie Jo said as the truck swerved in front of her, and time stood still for a moment. All sound was muffled around her as if she was underwater, but she heard loud and clear, "Seth is in my arms." It was so real and so convincing, she immediately exited the freeway and turned around to drive hours back to Cloverdale to tell my mom in person that she knew for a fact that Seth was safe in the arms of Jesus. She knew Seth was okay; she knew he was in the arms of Jesus. It was loud and clear, undeniable, and she had to share it with us. It was a sign; it was a gift.

With heavy hearts, my parents went to the local mortuary to finalize my brother's funeral plans. I cannot imagine the pain and agony they were feeling in that moment; it's hard to even think of. No one should have to face that. As they sat in the room feeling hopeless and broken, they began to look in a book for an urn; my father looked up and said, "You've got to be kidding me." As my mom looked up, they both were staring at a bronze urn with the most beautifully etched wolf. A detailed, brave, yet compassionate-looking wolf. As I mentioned above, Seth loved wolves *a lot*. Anyone who saw a wolf that knew and loved him immediately thought of him. How "random" is a wolf urn? How many other people love wolves this much? In a moment, that felt chaotic, unhinged, and out of place.

They were comforted with this urn so specific to Seth. It was a sign; it was a gift.

The day of my brother's service. My husband and I drove back to my parents with our two-year-old daughter Olivia. We pulled up to my parents' house and parked. We sat there for just a second; it had been an emotionally exhausting day. As we sat there, our toddler pointed in between our two front seat chairs and said, "There's Uncle Seth." She said it in a very simple, matter-of-fact, and emotionless way.

We said, "Awe, yeah." Then she pointed to the same spot and said, "There's Uncle Seth" in the same way. We acknowledged her again, not thinking much of it. She said it a third and fourth time, pointing to the same spot; we again acknowledged her. But after the fourth time, my husband and I looked at each other quizzically then looked back at her and said, "Where?"

She pointed again and said, "There's Uncle Seth."

We asked, "Outside?"

She said no with her eyes squinted, shaking her head like we were senseless. She pointed again and said, "There's Uncle Seth."

We asked, "Where do you see him?"

And she responded, "In the car next to my seat."

We looked at each other in shock. As we got out of the car, my husband said, "I don't know how, but Olivia just saw Uncle Seth." We went into the house to tell our family. My parents were not home yet. Those we told immediately felt comforted by our toddler's miraculous experience. The fact that it came from her was the sweetest part about it. She didn't even fully understand he was gone. Her experience was not attention-seeking or done with any mal intent. It was just a toddler stating a fact purely. When my parents got home, they were also comforted by Olivia's experience. My mom kept asking Olivia if she saw Uncle Seth and details about it. Olivia didn't answer any of the questions. Right before we left to go home that night, my mom asked her more straightforward questions. She asked, "Did you see Randy tonight?"

Olivia said, "Yes."

My mom asked, "Where?"

Olivia said, "At the restaurant."
She asked, "Did you see Jay tonight?"
Olivia said, "Yes."
My mom asked, "Where?"
Olivia stated, "At the restaurant."
My mom asked, "Did you see Uncle Seth tonight?"
Olivia said, "Yes."
My mom asked, "Where?"
Olivia said, "In the car next to my seat." We all just looked at each other in amazement. It was a sign; it was a gift.

A few weeks before my brother's accident, he was saying goodbye to my mom as she left his house. He leaned against his porch column and said, "My love transcends space and time," as he was saying goodbye from the visit. In that moment, my brother was dealing with depression and anxiety. So rightfully, it concerned my mom. She directly asked him, "What does that mean? You're not going to hurt yourself, are you?"

He smiled, laughed, and said no, as if she was silly for even thinking that's what he meant. (For those who have experienced loss in this way, I wholeheartedly believe there is infinite mercy for a heart hurting this badly. I know loved ones who have either ended their life or thought about it, and I know God is closely concerned with their pain. Eternity is always within grasps. Only God knows their heart, and I believe pursues them desperately until their final breath.) My mom told me of his words a little while after his accident when I was longing for him. After she told me the words, he spoke I started to read them in the books I was reading about heaven and NDE, not just once but numerous times in multiple books. He was not the only person who had a NDE and understood that we're always connected by love no matter how far away or physically removed we're from each other.

Many stories use that exact phrase: "Love transcends time and space" when describing their NDE and felt connection to loved ones. As if you just know once you experience it. Love and unity, both with God and loved ones, is a common theme understood by those who have had NDEs; John Burke's book *Imagine Heaven*, filled with many firsthand accounts of NDEs from all walks of life, repeats the importance of love and unity often in the individual stories told. Sometimes I feel Seth's love and his spirit with me now more than ever. I believe Seth said, "My love transcends time and space," not only because he understood the magnitude or the importance/emphasis placed on love and family from his NDE but also that there is always a connection even after leaving earth physically. After hearing he spoke those words, it made me wonder if he had an idea or sense that he would go to heaven at a young age.

After reading *To Heaven and Back* by Mary C. Neal, MD, I feel like my instinctual thought was confirmed. Often, as I processed in my grief, I had instinct or gut feelings come over me; I now believe it was the Holy Spirit or discernment nudging me in that direction. These instinctual feelings would be confirmed repeatedly and in the perfect moments. Knowing our love transcends time and space brought me so much comfort. We are and always will be connected and understand how loved we're by each other. He will always be my baby brother; we're not separated by time or space. To add to the series of confirmations, another book appeared on our doorstep, different from the ones I mentioned in chapter 2. To this day, I don't know who it's from, but it's titled *Journey Out of Time, A study of the interval between death and the resurrection of the body* by Arthur C. Custance. It came right at the time my mom told me what Seth had said and it stated, "Love transcends time and space" very quickly in the book, like several other books with stories of NDEs that I was reading at the time. These were signs; these were gifts.

A little while after Seth's accident, my mom found something in her journal that she did not remember writing. It was in her handwriting and dated close to his accident, but it did not sound like her. When reading it, it sounds like a letter or word from our heavenly father, it reads like this:

> I did it for him. It was his time.
> He needed to come home; his battle was over.
> The pain he felt was more than he could handle.
> I put his needs first like you asked.

You gave him to me; you wanted his best.
He needed to come home out of his storm.
He needed my peace and to know I forgave him
for all his sins.
He needed the love that could only come from me.
Now I hold him in my arms, and he feels no pain.
I want to do the same for you, my child.
I see you trying to be strong in your faith.
I know you don't see it now, but trust in me.
I have a plan for you, and there will be beauty
from these ashes.
You will see him again.

When I first heard these words from my mom's journal entry, I did not doubt its truths. I knew how much Seth struggled from carrying others' pain and being too hard on himself. The words reminded me of things Seth told me when sharing his NDE with me. He did long to feel complete peace and love again. And Bobbie Jo's word from God, Seth is safe in his arms. God granted us reassurance and continued reassurance with similar words, given in different ways, to different people. He really wanted us to know that Seth was not only okay but thriving as well. This was a sign; this was a gift.

For a couple years after Seth's accident, I would get beams of sunlight, a green orblike thing and/or rainbows in many of the pictures I took. I felt in my gut and heart that they were signs from God or Seth that he's okay, still with us somehow, saying a little hello. It was unreal how often they came up and in the shade or in the house. On his birthday, I would pray for rainbows and got one for three years straight, including a giant rainbow in a picture my friend Lorraine took of me and my girls in the shade on a hike for Seth on his birthday.

Speaking of being "surrounded," my friend Lorraine was/is such a gift to me. She has been a beautiful gift to my grieving heart. She spent countless hours with me my first couple years after Seth's accident. She knows grief and loss all too well after losing her father at a young age. She understood the pain and finality of death. She listened, showed up on every anniversary, encouraged, reassured me, and gave me a safe place to process.

A large rainbow appeared, under big trees without sunlight able to seep in, over our heads in every picture. You could not see anything with the naked eye, but every picture bright and obvious in the shade, there was a rainbow just over our heads. These pictures have slowed down a lot, and I rarely see them now. I sometimes questioned if it was a coincidence or if I was reaching for comfort. But my family and friends supported me in it, they would often send me pictures of rainbow or beams of sunlight. One of my best friends from college said she prayed for a rainbow as a sign that Seth was okay on his first birthday gone. She had moved to Oregon a year prior and said rainbows are rare that she had never seen one there. But she went for a walk and prayed for one anyway. She sent me a video on his birthday, ecstatic. A rainbow appeared a few min into her walk, and she was almost moved to tears. She said, "Well, hello, Seth, happy birthday, I see you." And recently, my friend who lost her aunt said, "I keep getting these green orblike things in all my pictures since my aunt passed. I almost jumped off her couch! I said the same thing happened to me the first couple years after Seth passed.

I believe they're signs telling us they're okay, and their love is still with us. There were too many "coincidences" to just be coincidences. Now, I fully disagree with the idea of a coincidence. I believe in an active and intentional God who knows our needs and is performing miracles big and small every day. Sometimes we're more in tune to receive them than other times, but God is always present and active in our needs. I believe these were all signs; I believe these were all gifts. I believe these were works of a miraculous God. We cannot put him in a box. There's nothing our God is incapable of, from his sweet whispers of reassurance, to parting the sea, to healing the sick, and even raising the dead. He's just that good!

ABIDE

Rattle
feat. Tasha Cobbs Leonard
Brandon Lake Bethel Music "House of Miracles"

My God is able to save and deliver and heal
and restore anything that He wants to
Just ask the man who was thrown on the bones of
Elisha if there's anything that He can't do
Just ask the stone that was rolled at the tomb in the
garden what happens when God says to move
You gotta move.

Jubilee
feat. Naomi Raine and Bryan and Katie Torwalt
Maverick City Music TRIBL (YouTube)

The spirit of the Lord is upon me
I'm anointed to bring hope
A promise fulfilled in the moment; I'm still watching it unfold
There's good news for the captive a proclamation for every soul
There are liberties for the broken an invitation to be made whole
Listen for the free man singing he's delivered me
Look out for the woman shouting His garment made me clean
Listen up the seasons changing He is rebuilding everything
Listen for the people shouting this is Jubilee
Can you hear it
This is Jubilee, I know it, I can hear it, I can feel it
There is true joy in His freedom
So, open your heart and receive it
There is a hope to believe in…Jesus
Can you hear it, this is, this is the sound of Jubilee
Listen
He's speaking, He's working, He's moving
He is still speaking
I was blind now I see, you delivered me
Hallelujah.

4

Personal Touch

Your Father knows what you need before you ask Him. (Matthew 6:8)

And my God will supply every need of yours according to His riches in glory in Christ Jesus. (Philippians 4:19)

He who did not spare his own son but gave Him up for us all, how will he not also graciously give us all things? (Romans 8:32)

Ask, and it will be given to you. Seek, and you will find; knock and it will be opened to you. (Matthew 7:7)

If you abide in me, and my word abides in you, ask whatever you wish, and it will be done for you. (John 15:7)

A dear friend recently lost her husband. Each day, she posts these heartbreaking yet beautiful notes about him, the things she misses and things that remind her of him throughout her day. Recently, she shared a story about how the "noisy old-fashioned clock" in their living room (that only her husband knew how to work and was loved most by him) stopped working down to the minute that he was called to be with Jesus. She also shared that when she called to reserve him a spot at the cemetery his grandparents were buried at the person on the other line stated they currently only had one spot available. The one spot left "happened" to be right below his grandparents—at the cemetery where her husband drove by in his bus often and would honk to say hello to his grandparents. This brought comfort to her grieving soul. Later, as she was visiting his grave site, one of the bus drivers from the company he managed drove by and honked. They did not know Rochelle was there visiting, but again, it comforted her grieving soul. Just as Justin, her husband, used to drive by and honk in honor of his grandparents, now his colleagues did the same in honor of him. As I read her stories of grief and though hard to see in the moment, stories of hope and reassurance, I am reminded of the *many* ways God reassured me. Reassurance that was so personal, so intricate, that the only rational explanation is God. A living God. A God who knows the depths of our souls. A God who is in the details. Her stories remind me of the gut-wrenching pain that is grief. But they also remind me of the intimacy and closeness of my Lord and Savior at that time.

One night, I lay in bed, sobbing. My husband was snoring next to me. I often try to wait until everyone is asleep to really "let it out." I was in so much physical pain and agony from the grief. I physically hurt everywhere in my body but especially in my chest. I would grip it as I cried because of the sharp pain that radiated as I cried. I did not know this type of pain was possible from grief. I lay sobbing. I wanted to let out my sadness and pain in words. I wanted to pray, but my prayers were just moans and sobs. Suddenly, after I'd been laying there feeling tortured for a while, my husband woke up from what sounded and seemed like a deep sleep. (My husband loves the Lord. He is a wise man and leads with a loyal faith, but he's a quiet, faithful man. He doesn't always pray out loud or express himself in words.) He stands up, walks over to my side of the bed, reaches out his hand, and begins to pray in the spirit. It was as if he was reading my soul. Not my mind, it was way more detailed and targeted. My mind was numb and felt like scrambled eggs. It was words from the deepest part of me. He would pray in tongues and then translate it and it was as if he had a map or script with all the answers and reassurance my soul needed in that very moment.

As he prayed, I felt a physical touch from God. A blanket of peace fell over me. My body and mind rested. My soul felt heard and reassured. My husband walked back to his side of the bed and went back to sleep with no other words. I was finally able to sleep for the first time in weeks. The next morning, I thanked him. I asked if he was aware that he prayed in tongues, a gift I have prayed for myself, he said, "Yeah." I asked if he had ever done that before. He said, "I don't know?" And that was that. We never really talked about it again. But I remember it as one of the most special moments between my husband and me. Never have I felt more loved or deeply cared for. It was so personal; only God knows the depths of our souls. He knows the small details and each of our stories. He doesn't just leave us to figure it out. He understands our pain and provides personal touches and reassurances to carry us through the most difficult of moments.

There were many times I would cry to God and pray about how I missed Seth, asking for help in my pain and longing. A lot of times when I would meet with God and just be real/vulnerable, holding nothing back I would feel the Holy Spirit so distinctly on the left side of my face. I never really knew what this meant and why just the left side of my face, but I knew it was there, and I was not alone.

Months later, while lying in bed crying, I felt this same presence on my left cheek/side of the face, and I asked God why. What does it mean why such a specific spot to embrace me? I wondered if it could be because that was the same side Seth injured in his accident? I fell asleep asking the question and crying. While sleeping, I had a very lifelike and vivid dream of Seth coming up behind me and kissing my left cheek. It felt so real, not like a dream. Then the kiss turned into the feeling I would get while being comforted by the Holy Spirit. The feeling was so strong it woke me up from a deep sleep. I woke up with my hand grabbing the left side of my face because the feeling of the Holy Spirit was so strong. And in that moment, I knew. When I felt the Holy Spirit comforting me in those moments of deep sadness and vulnerability, it was also in a sense a kiss from Seth. God's way of telling me even though he is not physically with me, his love is with me. He is and always will be my baby brother. Our "love transcends space and time."

As I processed this in prayer, I asked God if Seth prays for me now like I used to pray for him. I just had this sense that we switched roles in a way, and now it was my little brother worrying about me being okay. I asked and, in my gut, felt like I knew the answer; but the conversation ended there. I then decided to pick up my book *Heaven* by Randy Alcorn, and the next part I read talked about "prayers of the saints" (Revelations 5:8). Again a noncoincidental confirmation to my question. Confirmation sent in the perfect moment. Each time I had a question, I felt as if I knew the answer in my gut but needed reassurance, the same thought would come up in a book or a conversation at just the perfect time. Such a clever and masterful work of art is the mending of our Savior. Our Father in heaven, who is all-knowing, present, and wise, delivered again.

Someone very near and dear to Seth and us shared this with my mom and I one day:

> Today at work I looked over at my phone, and I don't know why, but I thought about how I am never gonna get a notification from Seth again. And some time later, like not even a few minutes later, I saw I had a missed call from a (707) area code, and I called back but it said, "Number not in service." I don't think it was a coincidence. I really think it was Seth telling me that he's still around and it made me feel better."

She knew it wasn't a coincidence in her gut. These are reassurances, gifts from a personal God. A God that knows what we need before we know we need it ourselves. A God who meets us where we're at and tends to our soul. I am so thankful for a God who chooses to abide in us so we can follow his lead and abide in him.

JAMIE MARIE OGIAMIEN (LAMPERT)

What a Friend We Have in Jesus
Lyric Video by Lydia Walker Acoustic Hymns

What a friend we have in Jesus
All our sins and griefs to bear
What a privilege to carry
Everything to God in prayer
O What Peace we often forfeit
O what needless pain we bear
All because we do not carry
Everything to God in prayer
Have we trials and temptations
Is there trouble anywhere
We should never be discouraged
Take it to the Lord in prayer
Can we find a friend so faithful
Who will all our sorrows share
Jesus knows our every weakness
Take it to the Lord in prayer
Are we weak and Heavy-laden
Cumbered with a load of care
Precious Savior still our refuge
Take it to the Lord in prayer
Do thy friends despise forsake thee
Take it to the Lord in prayer
In His arms He'll take and shield thee
Thou wilt find a solace there
What a friend we have in Jesus
All our sins and griefs to bear
What a privilege to carry
Everything to God in prayer.

ABIDE

"Sound Mind"
Bryan and Katie Torwalt, Sound Mind (Official Live Video)

In the chaos you're the peace
In my suffering you're here with me
In the darkness you never leave
God of mercy you're walking with me
I surrender anxiety
All the striving has to cease
In this moment you're still the King
This is a gift you're giving to me
A sound mind for the spirit of fear
A sound mind so that I can see clearly
A sound mind your spirit is here
A sound mind, a sound mind
Wash over me
There's a table where we meet, it's in the presence of my enemy
I will listen and I will feast on every word you're speaking to me
I remember who you are, you are my fortress and my God
I will stand in authority, in Jesus' name all the darkness will flee
A sound mind for the spirit of fear
A sound mind so I can see clearly
A sound mind your spirit is here
A sound mind, A sound mind
Wash over me, with your peace
Thank you, Jesus,
You saved healed delivered me, Jesus' blood washed over me
Command my soul awake arise, use each breath to prophesy
A sound mind for the spirit of fear
A sound mind so that I can see clearly
A sound mind your spirit is here
Every voice let it be your voice Jesus
Every lie of the enemy has to cease, even now
Wash over us with peace.

5

Dreams: Everything Will Be Okay

And afterwards, I will pour out my spirit on all people. Your sons and daughters will prophesy, your old men will dream dreams, your young men will see visions. (Joel 2:28)

We both had dreams. They answered, but there was no one to interpret them. Then Joseph said to them, do not interpretations belong to God? (Genesis 40:8)

But after he had considered this, an angel of the Lord appeared to him in a dream and said, Joseph son of David, do not be afraid to take Mary home as your wife, because what is conceived in her is from the Holy Spirit. (Matthew 1:20–23)

When they had gone, an angel of the lord appeared to Joseph in a dream. "Get up," he said, "take the child and his mother and escape to Egypt. Stay there until I tell you, for Herod is going to search for the child to kill him." (Matthew 2:13)

> After Herod died, an angel of the lord appeared in a dream to Joseph in Egypt. (Matthew 2:19)

> But god came to Abimelek in a dream one night. (Genesis 20:3)

> He said, "Listen to my words:" when there is a prophet among you, I, the lord, reveal myself to them in visions, I speak to them in dreams. (Numbers 12:6)

> To these four young men god gave knowledge and understanding of all kinds of literature and learning. And Daniel could understand visions and dreams of all kinds. (Daniel 1:17)

After Seth's accident, God sent dreams to multiple people but with a common theme; several people shared these dreams with me. The repetition was so comforting because I knew it wasn't a coincidence. They were gifts from God.

Seth's lifelong friend, Joey, told me he had a "very detailed, more real than life itself," dream of Seth after his accident. He said in his dream, he went into my parents' house knowing Seth was gone and feeling sad. As he walked into the office, he saw Seth standing there. He told me the details of what he was wearing at the time and how the office looked different than before. He said Seth was standing by the window and smiling big. He said Seth looked so happy and radiant. Because he wasn't expecting to see him after his accident, Joey said he semi collapsed in his dream, leaning against the wall by the office door and sobbed. He said as he sobbed, Seth came over and comforted him. He said Seth was smiling, stroking his head, and repeating over and over "everything will be okay."

I thanked Joey for sharing and told him he's not the first person who has had a "vivid, more real than life" dream where Seth said, "Everything will be okay." I told him I felt they were dreams or visions from God, and he wants us to know Seth is okay and everything will be okay. A couple of weeks later, Joey went to visit my parents to show his love and consideration for Seth and our family. He shared his dream with my mom and asked if he could see the office. When he walked into the office, he partially collapsed against the wall by the office door and began to sob. The office had been redecorated since he had last been there, but it was identical to his dream. God could have shown him Seth in any room in the house, but he chose the recently redecorated office as the setting for his dream. I believe to later confirm the validity of this surreal dream. I also believe as he was supported by the wall, crying, his dream in a way came to life again. I think Seth's spirit or the Holy Spirit was there comforting him, telling him, "Everything will be okay." When Joey later told me of this visit again, I was awestruck by the kindness and detailed work of God. First, the gift of a vision in a dream but to have it confirmed by the replication of the room weeks later something Joey couldn't have "dreamed" up on his own. God is good; everything will be okay.

My cousin Chelsi told me she had a dream that was "so real and vivid." She said Seth was wondering if it was his right time to go to heaven, and a little girl kept reassuring him, "Everything will be okay." When I asked what the little girl looked like, Chelsi tried to describe her as best as she could, and immediately, I knew who she was. A very close family member. Someone Chelsi had never met, so she would not have been able to describe her in such detail unless it was God. I knew, and I loved that that's the person God chose to comfort Seth and now us. God is good; everything will be okay.

We had other close friends and family come up to my mom and I who had dreams where they were so "vivid and real" and that Seth told them, "Everything will be okay." Each time a friend or family member shared this common-themed dream, they would also mention that Seth looked "healthier and happier than they have ever seen him." God is good, and he definitely wanted/wants us to know everything will be okay.

As we reflected on these gifts, the truth of them continued to sink in. It was in alignment with the other gifts and truths shared in other ways. My mom sat down to write out her testimony for a Bible study she had started in her home, something also started in honor of Seth, and realized this truth was a recurrent gift given to her even as a child. My mom grew up in a broken home with a lot of fighting between her parents. She did not feel safe as a kid. This affected her schooling, so they wanted to hold her back in school. Her parents decided to send her to Calvary Baptist rather than hold her back. This is where she learned about Jesus in chapel. She learned from Ms. Alexander that Jesus is there to protect her, so she asked Jesus into her life. And from then on, the fighting did not stop, but as she lay in bed at night, fearful, she felt a presence stroking her hair and would hear a repetitive whisper, "Everything will be all right." A soothing presence to comfort her in her fear, a presence to bring her peace when peace did not make sense. As she reflected on her testimony, the truth that was given to her then was connected to the truth and reassurance we were/are receiving now. God does not have to make these heart revelations tie together or so profound, yet he does. There is always a full circle when it comes to God and how he so intricately works. As a child in a home that felt unsafe, God wanted my mom to know he is with her and "everything will be all right." As an adult suffering from losing a child, something no parent should have to face, God likewise wanted her to know he is with her and "everything will be okay," not just for her but for her beloved son as well. I am thankful for this truth, and how God gifted us over and over to confirm He's working in our suffering and has victory in the end.

Be Alright
Evan Craft, Danny Gokey, and Redimiz
Lyrics from https://www.azlyrics.com

There's a name that can silence every fear
There's a love that embraces the heartache, the pain and the tears
Through my faith and my doubting
I know one thing for sure
His word is unfailing
His promise secure
Todo va a estar bien

JAMIE MARIE OGIAMIEN (LAMPERT)

Everything will be alright
The whole worlds in His hands
Your whole worlds in His hands
In the darkness and the trials, He's faithful and He is true
The whole world is in His hands
Y toto va estar bien
Everything will be alright
Father, you say everything is gonna be alright
But my circumstances say I won't last through the night
I need your word to hold me now, I need you to pull be through
I need a miracle, a breakthrough, I need you
They say you hold the whole universe in your hands
But my world is falling apart like it's made of sand
Am I small enough to slip through the cracks
Can you take my broken pieces and put them back
Give me faith to believe you are on my side
Open my eyes to see you working in my life
Let the past remind me you never fail
Tell my soul it is well.

6

Patient and Kind

May the Lord direct your hearts to the Love of God and to the steadfastness of Christ. (2 Thessalonians 3:5)

But the fruit of the spirit is love, joy, peace, patience, kindness, goodness and faithfulness. (Galatians 5:22)

The Lord is compassionate and gracious, slow to anger, abounding in love. He will not always accuse, nor will he harbor his anger forever; he does not treat us as our sins deserve or repay us according to our iniquities. (Psalm 103:8–10)

But when the kindness and love of God our Savior appeared, he saved us, not because of righteous things we had done, but because of his mercy. He saved us through the washing of rebirth and renewal by the Holy Spirit, whom he poured out on us generously through Jesus Christ our Savior. (Titus 3:4–6)

> Because your love is better than life, my lips will glorify you. (Psalm 63:3)
>
> Therefore, as god's chosen people, holy and dearly loved, clothe yourselves with compassion, kindness, humility, gentleness and patience. (Colossians 3:12)
>
> How priceless is your unfailing love, O god! People take refuge in the shadow of your wings. (Psalm 36:7)

Even with God's frequent reassurance, doubt crept in. The enemy comes to steal, kill, and destroy, and he doesn't relent. But God! He comes to give life in abundance, so he will not leave us stuck if we rely on him. There were several moments I remember in detail where Satan tried to steal my hope in eternity and my joy in God's reassurance, but God stepped in with such patience and kindness toward me and triumph against the enemy.

I am a night-shift labor and delivery nurse, and as I was driving to work one night, I was crying on the way to work. This was my normal routine at the time. I rarely had dry eyes, especially when alone. And that drive, in particular, sometimes made me angry because it reminded me of Seth driving in the ambulance at night on the same freeway going the same direction. So I began to become angry and question God: "Why did you allow this? He was so young. So much life. Why didn't you take me instead? I am his older sister. I was supposed to protect him. Why? Why? Why?"

Then I heard God speak with gentleness and zero judgment. He posed the question, "Would you send Olivia to die violently on the cross to guarantee Seth's eternity?" Immediately I felt gut-punched. My first thought was, *Oh no, I could never imagine Olivia dying in such a gruesome way*. It was painful to even consider for a second. Then I questioned myself, "Jamie, a moment of suffering in exchange for Seth's eternity?"

I responded, "I can't even think of Olivia going through that. I would gladly send myself."

And God answered in such kindness and patience again. He said, "That is how much I love your brother. What you can't even think about, I did." And without God speaking another word, I knew all in one moment, he loves Seth more than I can fathom. I thought my love for him was big, but not compared to God's. He is not a God who "wastes." He loved him enough to send his one and only son to die a brutal death on the cross to guarantee Seth's eternity. That kind of sacrificial love doesn't need to be questioned. He did the unthinkable to guarantee Seth's eternity, and surely, Seth is in good and loving hands now.

Another time I was in the shower, again, alone, so I was able to cry freely; and I started asking why again. "Why him? Why not me?" And I actually heard God giggle at me. And again, in a moment, my soul was reminded of this car drive. God's amusement was not mocking or degrading; it was gentle. As if he was saying, "Jamie, again, remember how much I love?" I couldn't help but laugh/cry myself. How much reassurance do I need? But I knew God was not angry with my human ways, slightly amused, but not angry.

Another time, I was joyfully sharing with a friend who also believes all the ways God has reassured me of Seth's salvation. I shared some of the personal encounters from God that I have experienced and that were shared to me by others. My friend received it well and was a kind, listening ear but at one point in the conversation asked if Seth was baptized in water.

I said, "No, I don't think so," and they said they believed that was a requirement for heaven. I don't think I was aware prior to that conversation that some churches believe water baptism to be a requirement for salvation. Immediately, doubt crept in. Satan knows how to take small interactions or words not intended to hurt and twist them. I began to pray and web search this thought. That's when I learned some churches hold this belief. But God spoke again with patience and kindness. He spoke moreso in a thought or quick understanding, not exact words. But I felt a sense of him saying, "Jamie, when will you trust the discernment I have given you? When a pastor told you I couldn't give visions or dreams, doubt crept in. When a friend says Seth needs water baptism for eternity, doubt crept in. I know confidence in knowledge is an insecurity of yours. I know you feel 'less than' because you're not a pastor or spiritual leader, because you did not grow up in a Christian home, or because you struggled in school, etc. But I have given you the gift of discernment. My spirit lives in you. My power is strong in your weakness. Listen to what I have spoken to you. You do not need man's approval. Your pastor and fellow believers are human too. No one has all the answers. Trust what I have spoken to you." Such patience and kindness as my father in heaven reassured me once again.

Before that following Easter, on Good Friday, I was holding my youngest, Brooklyn, and watching my oldest, Olivia, dance. I felt overwhelmed with love and adoration. I was praying and thanking God for the gift of the cross. Thanking him for eternity and the opportunity for my family to all be reunited again one day. I thanked him for my beautiful girls and the fact that they will get to be with Uncle Seth one day. I looked at both girls and said, "I would go through life and HG a million times for this moment with you." As I said that out loud, I heard God. He was saying, "Same, Jamie, same. I would go through my life of suffering, ridicule, and death on the cross a million times for this moment with you." I felt this word as a word to extend to all his children in that moment. My depth of love for my beautiful girls immediately translated to his love for me and all of his children. It was an aha moment. God's love, patience, and kindness is so very vast. I can only begin to understand how good it is.

Good Good Father
Tony Brown and Pat Barrett (musixmatch.com)

Oh, I've heard a thousand stories of what they think you're like
But I've heard the tender whisper of love in the dead of night
and you tell me that you're pleased and that I'm never alone
You're a good, good father
It's who you are

ABIDE

And I am loved by you
It's who I am
Oh, and I've seen many searching for answers far and wide
But I know we're all searching for answers only you provide
Cause you know just what we need before we say a word
Because you are perfect in all of your ways
Oh, it's love so undeniable
I, I can hardly speak
Peace so unexplainable
I, I can hardly think
As you call me deeper still
You're a good, good father
It's who you are
And I'm loved by you
It's who I am
You are perfect in all of your ways.

Worthy of my Song
(Worthy of it All)
Feat. Phil Wickham and Chandler Moore,
Maverick City Music (YouTube)

I'm gonna sing till my heart starts changing
O I'm gonna worship till I mean every word
Cause the way I feel, and the fear I'm facing
Doesn't change who you are, or what you deserve
I give you my worship, you still deserve it
You're worthy of my song, I pour out your
praises in blessing and breakage
You're worthy, you're worthy of my song
You're, yes you are Jesus
I gonna live like my King is risen, gonna preach
to my soul that you've already won
And even though I can't see it, I'm gonna keep
believing that every promise you made is
as good as done

JAMIE MARIE OGIAMIEN (LAMPERT)

I give you my worship, you still deserve
it, you're worthy, you're worthy
You're worthy of my song
I'll pour out my praises in blessing and breakage
When I sat by that hospital bed you were worthy
As she could barely lift her head you were worthy
After all those tears were shed you were worthy
I'll never stop singing your praise
In the blessing and in the pain, you're worthy
Whether you say yes or no or wait you're worthy
And through it all I choose to say, you're worthy
I'll never stop singing your praise, I'll never stop singing your praise
And when I finally see your face, I'll cry worthy
And when you wipe those tears away, I'll cry worthy
Above every other name you're worthy,
I'll never stop singing your praise
I give you my worship, because you still deserve it
You're always worthy of my song, forever worthy of my song
This is my story, this is my song, praising my savior all the day long
In the valley I'll sing your praise
On the mountain I'll sing your praise
In sickness I'll sing your praise
In health I'll sing your praise
When I am poor, I'll sing your praise
When I'm whole I'll sing your praise
I've made up my mind, I will bless the Lord in all, come what may
You could throw anything at me, though he afflicts me,
yet will I trust, yet will I pray. You're worthy of it all
From you are all things, and to you are all things
You deserve the glory
I've never seen Him fail, blessed be the name of the Lord.

7

Love Not of This World

The Lord is not slow to fulfill His promise as some count slowness, but is patient toward you, not wishing that any should perish, but that all should reach repentance. (2 Peter 3:9)

If I speak in the tongues of men and of angels, but have not love, I am a noisy gong or a clanging cymbal. And If I have prophetic powers, and understand all mysteries and all knowledge, and if I have all faith, so as to move mountains, but have no love, I am nothing. If I give away all I have, and if I deliver up my body to be burned but have no love, I gain nothing. Love is patient and kind, love does not envy or boast; it is not arrogant or rude, it does not insist on its own way; it is not irritable or resentful; it does not rejoice at wrongdoing but rejoices with the truth. Love bears all things, believes all things, hopes all things, endures all things. Love never ends. (1 Corinthians 13:1–13)

For God so loved the world that he gave his one and only son, that whoever believes in him

> shall not perish but have eternal life. For God did not send his Son into the world to condemn the world, but to save the world through him. (John 3:16–17)
>
> The Lord is compassionate and gracious, slow to anger, abounding in love. (Psalm 103:8)

Throughout the process of receiving these gifts from God in the form of words, dreams, visions, and miracles, my understanding of his mercy and love has transformed. I always heard growing up in the church, "It's not by works but by faith you have been saved." Or "there is nothing we can do or say that will separate us from the love of God." And that "if you believe in your heart and confess with your mouth that Jesus died for our sins, you will have eternity with him." But our human tendencies allow pride, doubt, insecurities, and lies to control our thoughts and actions. I sometimes feel embarrassed that I questioned my brother's salvation. I know it was from a protective big sister heart, not a heart of judgment, but who am I? He believed in his heart, he confessed with his mouth, and his heart was sincere; he is saved! Life is messy. Satan is deceiving and sly. Satan has half of us thinking we're not good enough and never will be while the other half thinks they can and will earn their salvation. But in actuality, we complicate something that is meant to be so simple. God took care of it once and for all when he did the "unthinkable."

I love how my pastor, Thomas Craig, explains the "narrow road" when preaching on Matthew 7:13–14 ("Enter through the narrow gate. For wide is the gate and broad is the road that leads to destruction, and many will enter through it. But small is the gate and narrow is the way that leads to life, and only few will find it"). He explained it so well; the road is not narrow because it's exclusive. "Come to me, ALL you who are weary and burdened, and I will give you rest" (Matthew 11:28). And John 3:16, "That WHOEVER believes in me (Jesus) shall not perish but have eternal life."

The "narrow way" is, in a sense, exclusive—for those who believe in and choose Christ; but it's also the most inclusive—*all* and *whoever* are welcome! But it is indeed narrow as my pastor so wisely explained. This is because he described it as a way of affliction, affection, and a single one way; there is no other way—no middle road, easy road, or man-made way.

He went on to explain,

> The narrow way is a way of affliction because the narrow way is hard. It is a difficult path. Not many people are willing to pick up their cross and follow Christ or to put their hand to the plow and keep their eyes ahead of them. Jesus told a zealous man looking to be a disciple to go and sell all he had and come and follow him and the man went away because he could not give up his possessions. Why would anyone want to travel this narrow way in being a Christian if it seems to be filled with such affliction? New Christians are often surprised that their lives are not trouble free once they decide to follow Jesus.

He went on to explain and stated Ellicott's Bible commentary saying the term *narrow* literally means "pressed, or hemmed in between walls or rocks, like the pathway in a mountain gorge." And 1 Peter 4:12–13 warns us, "Dear friends, do not be surprised at the painful trial you are suffering as though something strange were happening to you. But rejoice that you participate in the sufferings of Christ, so that you may be overjoyed when his glory is revealed." "The Lord gets his best soldiers out of the highlands of affliction" (Charles Spurgeon). Just as Jesus demonstrated, the Christian life if full of affliction, it's narrow and hard. But

> [t]he narrow way is a way of affection, because the life of a Christian is thoroughly and completely a life of love. Brotherly love is the defining characteristic of a Christian, because love is the defining characteristic of God. It is our

own foolishness that says I must do this or that to get God to love me. We think this way because we are prone to love others based on conditions. How often have we worked for the love of others? We do what they want us to in order to make them happy so we can gain their approval. That is conditional love. The Love of God is unconditional. There simply is nothing you can do to make God love you more and there is nothing you can do to make him love you less. 1 John 4:8 'Whoever does not love does not know god, because God is love.' The narrow way is a way of love! Sometimes when we're afflicted, we think that God has forgotten us. We think that he cares about everyone else's pain, everyone else's situation but for some reason you believe that he has forgotten about you. You may think that being perfect will make God love you. It may surprise you to know that the apostles were not perfect men either. At one point, Paul approved of the murder of Christians, Peter denied knowing Jesus. Thomas doubted Jesus' resurrection. And the Old Testament servants didn't fare any better. Moses murdered a fellow Hebrew, King David lusted after his friend's wife and committed adultery with her and then essentially had him murdered to have his wife for himself. Noah was found drunk and passed out on the floor naked by his sons. If you were to accuse any of these men of God for these specific things, you would not be wrong. It should give us some comfort to know that even the most devoted disciples were no more worthy of God's love than you or me. God is love. The narrow road is a road of unconditional love.

Lastly, the narrow way is narrow

because it's the only way. There are many people who know of the story of Jesus, they know a little about the church and stories of the Bible, but mere knowledge about those things, no matter how good, cannot and will not lead a man to life. Billy Sunday once said, "Going to church doesn't make you a Christian any more than going to a garage makes you an automobile." I wonder how many people have a false sense of security based on their mere knowledge of spiritual things? Yes, Christianity is narrow; Jesus said it plainly. John 14:6 "I am the way, and the truth, and the life. No one comes to the father but by me." There is only one way to eternal life. There is only one way to eternal peace. There is only one way to eternal happiness. There is only one way to eternal security. The narrow way is the only way and the only way is through Jesus Christ the son of God! Regarding the narrowness of Christianity, one of the best phrases I've heard is: inclusive exclusivity. Yes, it is exclusive. It is only through Jesus. But Jesus also gave an invitation to "ALL" Matthew 11:28 and "WHOEVER" John 3:16. Consider the thought that Tim Keller posts in Making Sense of God: "A salvation earned by good works and moral effort would favor the more able, competent, accomplished and privileged. But salvation by sheer grace favors the failed, the outsiders, the weak, because it goes only to those who know salvation must be by sheer grace." That is what God's true love offers—this is a beautiful inclusive exclusivity—open to everyone—received only by faith/trust in Jesus, not human effort.

I now personally believe once saved, always saved. Although we may stray, he leaves the ninety-nine for the one. He *never* gives up on us and rejoices when we're found. Psalm 23, the verse read over my brother as he breathed his last breath, "Surely his goodness and mercy will follow me all the days of my life." The original text reads, surely, his mercy and goodness chases or pursues me all the days of my life. It's an active pursuit of love, mercy, and kindness. Strip away pride, doubt, guilt, and shame. They're lies; they're not true of God's children. We need to walk and live in the truth that we're actively pursued; our loved ones are actively pursued by a personal, powerful, and loving God. It is not by works. It is not earned. Everyone is welcome. It's a free gift of unconditional love and acceptance. All we have to do is receive this gift with a sincere heart, and his love will begin to transform us. Everyone's transformation looks different. It does not mean we will be perfect. But we can continue to walk in grace, and God's unconditional love will prove to the most transformative power in the world. "And I am certain that God, who began the good work within you, will continue his work until it is finally finished on the day when Christ Jesus returns" (Philippians 1:6).

My understanding of his love has transformed in such a tremendous way, and, I know I am only seeing the "tip of the iceberg," if you will, a still very distorted view. But, I firmly believe, not only, once saved always saved, but, also, the idea that God makes himself and eternity as easily accessible as possible. I would not make my children jump over hurdles to spend eternity with me. I long for that with every fiber of my being. I would do anything for them in order to make that happen. That's what our holy and just father did for us. The "unthinkable" in order to achieve what he longs for, an eternity of unity with us, his children. He made it happen. He has the ultimate victory. And while the enemy tries to tear us from that truth, God actively chases us down and lovingly pursues us in this imperfect life.

I cannot wait to see the full picture. God's tapestry of love, what a sight it will be when we can see all the broken pieces put back in place. All because of his loving-kindness. His free gift of eternity. Satan wants us to walk in the lies, walk in fear and doubt. He wants our pride and insecurities to result in us questioning our identity in Christ and ultimately steal the best gift ever offered to us. But looking back on God's pursuit of Seth, I am thankful God has allowed me to see pieces of the tapestry for Seth's life and our relationship beautifully pieced together. The masterfulness of his artistry has left me awestruck once again. God's love is an out-of-this-world kind of love. We can't fully comprehend it, but I am so thankful that in my anger, grief, doubt, questioning, shame, insecurities, fear, and prone to a wandering heart; the artist still gave me glimpses of this always pursuing, out-of-this-world kind of love. I hope to share this heart revelation with others throughout life.

The One You Love
Brandon Lake, Dante Bowe, and Chandler Moore, Maverick City Music

I can be real with you
Say anything and not be afraid
You made me and you like what you made
You made me and you don't make mistakes
You take me just as I am
You choose me all over again
Because I am the one you love
I don't have to prove anything
There's room at your table for me
Because I am the one you love
I know you're proud of me, even though
I don't deserve it sometimes
No, I'm not a perfect child
But I still make my father smile
I know you're proud of me
You take me just as I am
You choose me all over again
I know you love me, the real me
You know everything, and you still love me
They'll leave over a rumor, but you stay with the truth

JAMIE MARIE OGIAMIEN (LAMPERT)

Your love never fails
It's so consistent
You gave your life for me
You take me just as I am
I don't have to prove anything
Your love never fails
In the morning, in the evening… it never fails
In my lowest I've seen that your love never fails
Always pursuing me, even though I am not worthy
Always chasing me, even though I am undeserving
But you call me friend
You call me brother
How can this be the King, my friend
In all His holiness, still my friend
Even though He's perfect
Closer than a brother, mother or a father
In all His greatness, His holiness still my friend
I know that I can call on Him when I need Him
No matter how far I fall
No matter what I have done
He's still my friend
He still calls me His favorite
He saw my needs
I cry out to the Lord, and He heard my cry
I can call on Him when I need Him
Jesus is on the main line
Never too busy to answer His son or daughters
He's not in a hurry
He's never too busy
He never sleeps or slumbers.

ABIDE

Wouldn't It Be Like You
Bryan and Katie Torwalt, official live video (YouTube)

I thought I had you figured out.
So sure, I knew exactly how you'd move.
Thought my savior was coming with a sword in
His hand, to my surprise he came as a child.
Wouldn't it be like you to be different than we thought
Different than we want, but better.
You're better.
And wouldn't it be like you to be different than we thought
Different than we want, but better.
Yes, you are.
They left my savior in a tomb; hope was lost
and the dark was breaking through.
When you broke the bread and saw the holes in your
hands, how did I not see Son of God is Son of man.
Help me be like Mary laid out poured out I won't miss you in
a crowd because I love your voice and I know the sound.
And Jesus if it's you on the water in a cloud I'll be the first one
to walk out because I know your voice and I love the sound.
You're everything I need
Everything I'm lacking
Everything I need
Everything I'm lacking
Hold on, don't grow tired, don't give up, He's better.
We're thankful, and we're grateful
That He's better
Wouldn't it be like you to be different than we
thought different than we want but better.
Gratitude, so grateful.
Hold on, don't grow tired, don't give up
He's better.
We've only just seen a glimpse, He's better.

8

Made in His Image

Then God said, let us make mankind in our image, in our likeness, so that they may rule over the fish in the sea and the birds in the sky, over the livestock and all the wild animals, and over all the creatures that move along the ground. So, God created mankind in his own image, in the image of God he created them; male and female he created them. (Genesis 1:26–31)

For you created my inmost being; you knit me together in my mother's womb. I praise you because I am fearfully and wonderfully made; your works are wonderful; I know that full well. (Psalm 139:13–18)

For this is the covenant that I will make with the house of Israel after those days, declares the Lord: I will put my law within them, and I will write it on their hearts. And I will be their God, and they shall be my people. And no longer shall each one teach his neighbor and each his brothers, saying, Know the Lord, for they shall all know me, from the least of them to the greatest,

> declares the Lord. For I will forgive their iniquity, and I will remember their sin no more. (Jeremiah 31:33–34)

As God cared for me in my grief, I began to notice symbolic gestures and simple things that spoke to my grieving soul, gestures that we quickly may archive as coincidences. No, I absolutely do not believe in the notion of a coincidence anymore. These gestures or gifts were/are intentional; and I believe I noticed, in part, because of the fact that we are made in the image of God. I spoke briefly in a previous chapter about light and rainbows seen frequently in pictures or with the naked eye, especially the first year after losing Seth and often on anniversaries, birthdays, or on special occasions. Friends and family sent pictures to me of rainbows on Seth's birthday, the anniversary of his accident, or when they were simply thinking of him; and one appeared. On the day of his service, family and friends from out of town sent us or posted pictures of a large rainbow over our small town as they exited the freeway. People would post pictures of rainbows and say, "I see you, Seth." My heart was immediately drawn to them. I felt they were a little love letter from God or Seth sent from heaven, in order, to let me know he was okay. God continued to confirm these gifts as gifts, not coincidences in my heart. And I later connected just as rainbows were symbolic to me; they're extremely symbolic biblically. The Bible talks about their significance. In Genesis 9:13–16, God uses a rainbow to symbolize his covenant of forgiveness and love even while fully aware of our wandering hearts and sinful nature as humans, a symbolic gesture from God to symbolize his mercy and kindness knowing full well of our shortcomings both past and present. In Ezekiel 1:28, when Ezekiel has a vision of God, a rainbow is used to symbolize God's glory and light. Since we're made in his image, it's no wonder we instinctually are drawn to and reassured by their presence, and it's no wonder we are comforted by symbolic gestures.

Likewise, Seth, myself, and many others are very drawn to jewels and precious stones/crystals. I used to think it was human vanity that drew us to them, but now I think it's the fact that we're made in the image of God. Nothing God says, does, or makes is a coincidence or without care/thought. God created everything good; we're drawn to his creation. The Bible only warns us against worshipping anything but God. It does not tell us that we cannot enjoy what God has intentionally created. There is intentionality and symbolism in even the smallest of things. The Old Testament speaks of precious stones and their symbolic uses:

In Joshua 4:1–8, God miraculously parted the Jordan River, and as the Israelites crossed, Joshua led the twelve tribes to remove boulders from the riverbed, with which they make a symbolic memorial in order to remember God's love and miraculous assistance. The Bible lists a different gemstone for each of the twelve tribes of Israel. And in Exodus 28, God has Moses instruct them that the priest should wear a breastplate with the twelve precious stones representing the twelve tribes while performing priestly duties.

As I read books on heaven, one book that stood out while processing our likeness to God in terms of symbolism in creation is *Heaven* by Randy Alcorn. My heart had this revelation: We like precious stones because we're made in the image of God. We are reassured by rainbows and symbolic gestures because we're made in the image of God, made in his likeness. His truths are written on our heart. The Bible talks about the twelve precious stones of the tribes of Israel and how the walls of heaven are made of these precious stones. It also talks about how the stones all together make the colors of the rainbow. Since there were so many rainbows the week of Seth's service, me and many others without collaboration felt they were little hellos from Seth and, or, reassurances from God. And the more I learn about their significance biblically, I think now they could have possibly been sent straight from the walls of heaven.

Revelations 21 and 22 give us a taste-tester of heaven through symbolism, metaphors, and analogies. I believe these verses are purposefully vague because we just cannot fully understand the vastness of God and what's to come when we leave our earthly bodies and arrive in our forever home, heaven. In chapter 21 verses 9–21 the new Jerusalem is described to "gleam with the splendor of God. Its radiance was like that of precious stone, like jasper, clear as crystal.

The walls/foundation made with all 12 precious stones." (The Greek word for *foundation* is plural). "And the streets made of gold."

God opened my eyes and gave me reassurance in the form of symbolic gestures while grieving. I now realize this is something humans do a lot and are frequently comforted by. I see this in other first accounts of grief. Mary C. Neal, MD, writes in her book *To Heaven and Back* about being reassured by symbolic gestures. One gesture that she speaks about that comes to mind now is the blossoming of flowers. Flowers that don't normally grow where she lives, in her front yard, the same flowers that were most loved by the person she was grieving. I guess deep down, I've known this is a thing we do as humans, whether it be precious stones, numbers, flowers, rainbows, birds, etc. I believe we all do it to an extent. I just never connected the fact that we do this because we're made in his image. Part of our proof that this is instinctually a "human thing" is that the Bible is full of symbolism, which is the living word of God, and he is intentional in all things.

I ended up naming my daughter, who I was three months pregnant with during Seth's accident, Brooklyn. Her name was symbolic to me and reminded me of the verses in Revelations 22:1–2. A stream or brook of water flowing from the thrown of God. I was so intrigued with heaven at the time; I loved that her name reminded me of these glimpses of heaven where my brother is at peace and is fully loved. My grief counselor at the time, who was an angel on earth for me, also pointed out how symbolic it was that my daughter was born on August 12, with 8 being the symbol for eternity and 12 symbolizing not only the twelve biblical stones, which make up the walls of heaven and colors of the rainbow, but also the beautifully described tree of life on each side of this river in Revelations 22, flowing from the thrown of God bearing twelve crops of fruit to symbolize the twelve tribes of Israel and the healing of the nations.

I think when we're desperate enough to heal or find hope our eyes and hearts are opened more fully. Some might say these are just coincidences. But I believe they're intentional, symbolic gestures (movement or a sign) from a living and active God. I believe our God is in the smallest and biggest of details, and we're made in his image/likeness. These truths are engraved on our hearts. And he gives us a glimpse of his detailed splendor while on this side of heaven. One day, we will see his full splendor, and it will be both glorious and unfathomable.

Promises
Joe L. Barnes and Naomi Rain-Maverick City
Music (partial quote from YouTube)

Faithful through the ages
God of Abraham
You're the God of covenant and faithful promises
Time and time again, you have proven you do just what you said
Though the storms may come, and the winds
may blow, I'll remain steadfast
And let my heart learn, when you speak a word, it will come to pass
Great is your faithfulness to me
From the rising sun to the setting same, I will praise your name
The seasons change, you remain the same
God from age to age, though the earth may
pass away, your word remains the same
Your history can prove there's nothing you
can't do, you're faithful and true
Your faithfulness never runs out
I put my faith in Jesus, my anchor to the ground
My hope and firm foundation, He'll never let me down
My only hope, He'll never let me down
Great is your faithfulness to me
From the rising sun to the setting same, I will praise your name
In every season
My hope and firm foundation
Great is your faithfulness
In every season
Yes, I will bless you
In the middle of a storm
In the middle of my trial

ABIDE

I'll still bless you
In the middle of the road, When I don't know which way to go
I'll still bless you
I've got a reason to bless your name
You've been so faithful, you've been so good to me
Great is your faithfulness to me.

9

Beauty from Ashes

And provide for those who grieve in Zion—to bestow on them a crown of beauty instead of ashes, the oil of joy instead of mourning, and a garment of praise instead of a spirit of despair. (Isaiah 61:3)

Therefore, my dear brothers and sisters, stand firm. Let nothing move you. Always give yourselves fully to the work of the Lord, because you know that your labor in the Lord is not in vain. (1 Corinthians 15:58)

When the perishable has been clothes with the imperishable, and the mortal with immortality, then the saying that is written will come true: Death has been swallowed up in victory. Where, O death, is your victory? Where, O death, is your sting? (1 Corinthains 15:54–55)

So do not fear, for I am with you; do not be dismayed, for I am your God. I will strengthen you and help you; I will uphold you with my righteous right hand. (Isaiah 41:10)

> Greater love has no one than this: to lay
> down one's life for one's friends. (John 15:13)

While my brother's accident is tragic, beyond difficult, and life-altering, I did see some good come from a situation I do not wish on anyone. Though I will never know for sure, like I said in a previous chapter, I believe my brother died a hero, trying to protect another life. Knowing him, I do not think he could have lived with himself if anything happened to his passenger, and he lived. I also think if he was bedridden for the rest of his life, it would have clashed majorly with his free-spirited personality. He loved to help others. I believe God's mercy was weaved in and through that tragic night. My gut tells me, as well as firsthand stories from the incident/his injuries, that Seth died trying to protect his passenger (John 15:13). He would be proud of that, and God protected him from a life of regret and pain.

Some of his friends' lives were impacted positively as a result of his life and his love. A friend of his shared with me how he was numbing himself with alcohol right up until Seth's passing. He was arrested while under the influence, so after Seth's accident and this incident, he decided to turn his life around and become sober for his wife and kids. He started going to church where he met his arresting officer for the second time; he also "just so happened" to go to that church. The police officer showed him respect and tough love when he arrested him and continued to show the same compassion when "randomly" meeting at church. This same friend met with me after Seth's accident to let me know the impact Seth had on his life. He apologized for making Seth's life harder, his last couple years on this side of heaven. He talked about Seth's love and how he always loved him even at his worst as well as give him a place to live when he had nowhere else to go.

Another friend of his shared how he almost took his own life as a result of losing Seth "a brother, uncle to his girls, and someone who loved wholeheartedly." He wrote,

> His death broke me to the point that I did
> not want to continue with my existence. So, I

stuck the barrel of my pistol to my face and as I was crying and everyone screaming to stop, I looked at my eldest daughter and the look on her face told me that this was not the answer. I felt the spirit of my friend come to me and help me put the gun down and I chose to live a beautiful life raising my children.

Now he chooses life and sobriety every day. He has turned his life completely around. Seth was always known for his deep, sacrificial love. Losing him left a big hole in a lot of people's lives. But I know he would be proud of this friend and is cheering him on as he navigates this tough yet beautiful life.

Another friend of his had been in jail since their senior year of high school. They always talked about when he was released, he and Seth would have a big meal together. Seth hated that he spent all that time in jail essentially because he would not "talk" and give information about someone he knew that committed a crime. Seth hated injustice, like our Creator. He stood up for the one in need like our Creator. Seth often sent him money, visiting and communicating often. He stayed close to him throughout.

When Seth passed, I decided to write a letter, out of love, to family and friends of both Seth and me. (I have attached this letter at the end of the book.) Many responded with thanks and shared positive feedback from hearing some of Seth and my story through the letter. I ended up sending the letter to my brother's friend who was in jail at the time because I knew he meant the world to Seth, and my goal was to reach everyone we loved. We began to talk and formed a friendship of our own, thanks to Seth. I love to be close to his friends and love/support them; it feels like a way to be close to Seth as well as honor him. We're still friends to this day, and when he was released, we had a big dinner with friends and family just a couple days later. We felt honored to be one of his first meals and fellowship encounters, just as he had promised Seth. We continued to have "family" dinners where we talked about life and Seth. I am so thankful for the ways his friends loved/love my brother and for their friendship now.

Another example, of God's mercy and kindness given the horrible circumstances, would be the mutual reliance and faith-building friendship between my lifelong friend Lorraine and me. I wrote about her briefly in a previous chapter. I was reminded by her, while driving home from a women's night at church together, just how intrinsically God worked through our tragedy to bring beauty from the wreckage for the two of us and how he continues to extend that beauty to our loved ones. Lorraine is the friend I talked about briefly who was such a strong presence and listening ear the years to follow Seth's accident.

Lorraine tragically lost her father to cancer when we were in the sixth grade, the day before 9/11. Lorraine and I had played sports together since we were little, and my heart was ruined when I heard of her loss. Being in the sixth grade, I did not know exactly how to show up for her other than praying for her, which I did often throughout junior high, high school, and college. She never left my heart or mind, but the Holy Spirit would impress her strongly on my heart on certain holidays, anniversaries, or randomly throughout the years. Lorraine was one of the many people I sent my "love letter" to after Seth's accident. There were certain people I was more afraid to send it to compared to others, many of which were the most excited or ready to receive. In hindsight, it was obvious that Satan did not want them to have it out of fear to their response, knowing their hearts were in a place to receive.

After sending Lorraine the letter, I felt a nudge to invite Lorraine to a prayer group I had recently started. Also, a result of losing Seth, something I might not have started otherwise. I was nervous to call Lorraine because I knew she believed in God, her family went to church regularly before her father passed, but I did not know where her heart was at now and if my invite would be offensive. When I called to invite Lorraine, she gladly and readily accepted. She went on to tell me that the night before receiving the letter she had prayed to God, her heart was ready to go back to church, and she asked him how to go about that. The next day, she received the letter and felt it was an answer to prayer so she was going to call me, but before she could, responding to the Holy Spirit, I called her. Lorraine went on to remind me, as we drove home that night, how God used losing Seth to give me the motivation and courage to be bolder. I reflected on that and told her it was a mutual blessing in the end because while her heart was looking for a way to return to Christ and the church; my heart was looking for a friend who knew and loved God who could understand. Not only does Lorraine understand grief, but being a lifelong friend who loved both Seth and I deeply, she understood me. And having her back in church, excited and ready to serve and learn, allowed for an even deeper understanding of our shared grief and faith. She was/is one of my number 1 go-to relationships in order to process and feel heard/seen. She went on to say that since she has returned to church, so has her brother and sister-in-law. So have the many friends she has invited. She reminded me that, her sister in law, along with her two nieces, were recently baptized, and she's not sure how or when that would have happened otherwise. God used a tragedy in our lives to bring hope and healing in others. She said having her relationship with Christ restored allowed her to be the support she needed to be for me, as well, as her husband when he lost his father, shortly after Seth.

Lorraine went on to say that my mom's Bible study has touched so many lives as well. She stated, "Like your letter, I believe her Bible study was motivated and inspired by Seth." Reflecting on all this with Lorraine really opened my eyes. I did not even think of all the ways God took something so tragic in our lives and allowed good to come from it. Lorraine and I both mentioned the idea "domino effect" when processing the turn of events. Lorraine's prayer was answered, my need for understanding/companionship was answered…but it goes much deeper than that. Looking back, you can see the other family and friends whose lives were affected by just Lorraine, my mom, and my desperate need to be close to Christ/share the good news with others. If it took us years to realize what God brought from our hurt and desperate need, imagine all the ways He's working that we can't see now with our limited perspective. If our small circle was affected so drastically, who else does that extend to? God is working in our midst; he does not allow suffering or pain in vain. There is a purpose, just like Christ's brutal death on the cross; there is and will be beauty from our ashes (Isaiah 61:3).

I believe not only did God protect Seth in many ways the night of his accident, but he also used our tragedy to awaken a sense of complacency or pride in those who loved him most. I know Seth's example of love without judgment or bias has touched many people including myself. Just as my heart has grown in the knowledge and understanding of how perfect God's love is. I know my brother's legacy of kindness and love that he inherited from our Creator will live on through his loved one. And one day, God will redeem and return all that has been stolen from us when we lost Seth here on earth.

Ruins
Joe L. Barnes and Nate Moore Maverick City
Music (partial quote from YouTube)

I look around and all I see are burning buildings baren trees
Hopelessness is starting to take over
Son of man, I know you see, the deepest depths unknown to me
You're planting seeds among the ashes
You rebuild
You restore
All that's broken
From the ruins
You redeem
You return
All that's stolen
From your children
That's what you do
So be still my anxious heart
All that is gone is never lost
Emmanual is here and He is faithful
So, I won't let my praises stop, singing from these rubble rocks
Because I know you're good and you're able
You rebuild
You restore

JAMIE MARIE OGIAMIEN (LAMPERT)

All that's broken
From the ruins
You redeem
You return
All that's stolen
From your children
That's what you do
You raise beauty from ashes
Yeah, that's what you do
You turn sorrow to gladness
Yeah, that's what you do
So, I give glory and honor for all that you do
I will sing hallelujah for all that you do
You rebuild
You restore
All that's broken
From the ruins
You redeem
You return
All that is stolen
From your children
Yeah, that's what you do.

Simple Kingdom
Bryan and Katie Torwalt (with Cody Carnes)
(Official live video in YouTube)

Your kingdom is simple, as simple as love.
You welcome the children; you stop for the one.
We want to see people, the way Jesus does.
Your kingdom is simple, Lord teach it to us.
Your kingdom is humble, as humble as death.
This King is a savior who gave His last breath,
So may we dye daily, our pride laid to rest.
His kingdom is humble, and the broken are blessed.
Hallelujah, hallowed be your name.

ABIDE

May we live and breathe your praise
Let all creation sing, o' the king of Heaven reign.
Your kingdom is coming, your kingdom is here.
Alive in our waiting, at work in our tears.
So come to us quickly, forever I pray.
Your kingdom is coming, Lord Jesus draw near.
Your kingdom is backwards, it flows in reverse
What you call a treasure, this world calls a curse
The small become great and the last become first
Your kingdom is backwards, Lord teach us to serve.
As it is in your kingdom, let it be with your church.
Hallelujah hallowed be your name
May be live and breathe your praise
Hallelujah let all creation sing, o the king of heaven reign.

10

Eternal Hope

"Then I saw a new heaven and a new earth, for the first heaven and the first earth had passed away, and there was no longer any sea. I saw the Holy City, the new Jerusalem, coming down out of heaven from God, prepared as a bride beautifully dressed for her husband. And I heard a loud voice from the throne saying, look! God's dwelling place is now among people, and he will dwell with them. They will be his people, and God himself will be with them and be their God. He will wipe every tear from their eyes. There will be no more death or mourning or crying or pain, for the old order of things has passed away...And he carried me away in the spirit to a mountain great and high, and showed me the Holy City, Jerusalem, coming down out of heaven from God. It shown the glory of God, and its brilliance was like that of a very precious jewel, like a jasper, clear as crystal. It had a great high wall with twelve gates, and with twelve angels at the gates. On the gates were written the names of the twelve tribes of Israel... then the angel showed me the river of the water of life, as clear as crys-

> tal, flowing from the throne of God and of the Lamb down the middle of the great street of the city. On each side of the river stood a tree of life, bearing twelve crops of fruit every month. And the leaves of the tree are for the healing of the nations. (Revelations 21–22)
>
> My Father's house has many rooms; if that were not so, would I have told you that I am going there to prepare a place for you? And if I go and prepare a place for you, I will come back and take you to be with me so that you also may be where I am. (John 14:2–3)
>
> I consider that our present sufferings are not worth comparing with the glory that will be revealed in us. (Romans 8:18)

Life is messy and hard. Grief is life-altering and never-ending. It's forever changing but never goes away. Grief is the cost of love. It's confusing and layered with many other emotions.

But what I learned firsthand is God is good and close to the brokenhearted. He is not a passive God, but he actively pursues and intentionally mends. He provides the people and things needed to survive in the "shadow of the valley of death." He knows what is best. His compassion and love cannot be matched. He would do the "unthinkable" a million times for a moment of intimacy with his child. He wants us all to be in unity with him. He longs for an eternity with his children. He made a way when there was no way. All we have to do is come, choose him. He abides in us so we can follow his lead and abide in him. When we do, it's the sweetest of relationships. Life will still be messy and hard; but there's a best friend, provider, father, savior, counselor, all-knowing, wise, empathetic, and close God who meets you where you're at and redeems even the darkest of situations. We may only get a glimpse of this redemptive power while here, but even that is so sweet and kind. One day, we will see in full and that will be a glorious day.

I always felt thankful for heaven and eternity; even as a kid, I would pray for my loved one's souls/eternity with more urgency than their physical present needs. I've always placed a lot of concern and thanksgiving on the gift of being united forever without pain, suffering, or tears. But after losing Seth, a large part of my heart left with him. I do not feel as if I'll ever be whole here on earth again. A piece of me left with him, and I cannot fully get that back while here. So now more than ever, my hope and identity are in Christ and his free gift of eternity. One of the stories I read about in *Imagine Heaven* by John Burke talked about a family that was in a car accident. The husband Jeff describes this tragic accident and his NDE like this:

> I was encircled with light, a bright white light that seemed to be energized with pure, unconditional love. I was calm. Peace infused this almost tangible light. I realized all the pain was gone. I was fine...
>
> Then I felt a familiar touch. I opened my eyes. Tamara was right next to me. She was real too. I could feel her. She was alive... I looked at her. I could feel everything. She was crying and upset. Why? Where were we? Was the crash a bad dream now? Or had I died? Had we both died? And where were the boys?
>
> I had read about experiences like I was having. Many people describe passing through a tunnel toward a bright light. That wasn't happening to me. I felt like I was in some kind of protective bubble. And I felt alive, not dead.
>
> "You can't stay here," Tamara said. "You have to go back. You can't be here."
>
> Why was she crying?
>
> "You can't come. You cannot stay here."

What did she mean I couldn't stay? I belonged there.

"You have to go!"

She was as real as ever. The thought of our boys raced through my head. Where were they? Were they here too? If I stayed, would Spencer be left orphaned? Where was Griffin?

"You have to go!" Tamara insisted. But I didn't want to go anywhere. It seemed odd to me that in that glorious bubble, she would be upset. Was it heaven? I didn't know, but it made my earthly existence seem like a foggy dream. What I was experiencing was far more real, far more tangible, and far more alive than anything I had ever known. I pulled Tamara to me tightly. She was tangible as well. I even felt her wet tears on my skin. I kissed her. That was real. I smelled her hair. Not in the earthly sense, but with senses that seemed to be tenfold what I had experienced before.

"You can't be here. You have to go," she sobbed.

It almost felt as if my course was set. I didn't want to go, but I also knew she was right. I was not meant to stay. I felt I had a choice, but something deep within me knew I had to go back to Spencer... I looked into Tamara's eyes, those crystal, sky-blue eyes. Everything in the universe was calling me back to Spencer, but I wanted to stay with her. And where was Griffin? I felt a warm tear roll down my face and fall from my upper lip.

"I have to go."

"I know."

I looked at her one more time, the love of my life, and the wife of my dreams. I leaned forward. Putting my forehead onto hers…

"I love you."

"I know."

The next thing Jeff heard was the haunting reality of Spencer crying in the backseat of the crashed SUV. Tamara and Griffin, were dead. As he came to, Jeff heard a question, echoed into every cell of his being. The question was simply, "To what degree have you learned to love?"

John Burke goes on to write:

> Love God, love people—forever
>
> One of the biggest struggles people have with heaven is the thought of being separated from the ones they love most. Yet it's not heaven, but the effects of a fallen earth that separate us. God created us for a love that lasts forever. Love has always been God's central theme, and as you'll see in the coming chapters, love is the only thing that makes sense of why God allows so much hurt and pain in the meantime.
>
> Jesus was once asked, "Teacher, which is the most important commandment in the law of Moses?" Jesus replied, "You must love the Lord your God with all your heart, all your soul, and all your mind.' This is the first and greatest commandment. A second is equally important: 'Love your neighbor as yourself.' The entire law and all the demands of the prophets are based on these two commandments" (Matthew 22:36-40 NLT). To love God first, and then to let him help us love those around us as much as we love ourselves—

that sums up the scriptures and the point of every command.

Those who get a glimpse of Heaven agree on one thing more than anything—love is the point of it all. In the presence of God, they experience a love words cannot explain, and the people of heaven seem to be filled with a light that is love. So if love and relationship is the goal of life on earth, why would we think God wants to tear that apart or take relationship away from us in Heaven? Nothing could be further from the truth.

Everything God claimed to have done through the prophets and through Jesus is for the sake of love—to restore people to a love relationship with God, so he can teach us to love one another as he loves us. He intends those relationships to last in Heaven, and even more, to find their fulfillment in Heaven. The greatest love we feel for children, a spouse, friends, or family on earth amounts to a teaspoon of love compared to the oceans we will experience together for eternity. The Old Testament prophets foretold it, Jesus demonstrated it, and those who have had a peek behind the veil consistently say the same thing— God is love, and Heaven will be the greatest reunion ever.

God is love. And he created family. He delights when we love him and one another well, that's what we're called to do. As John Burke stresses throughout his book *Imagine Heaven*, a common understanding among those who have had NDEs is we are called to and made for love, peace, and unity. We're created for an eternity with Christ and meant to be united with loved ones. It's a deep desire in every human heart, and it's because we're made in his image. One day, there will be no more tears, no more goodbyes, no more longing… We will be reunited with our maker. We will have complete peace and understanding alongside our loved ones in our house in heaven.

Fear Is Not My Future
Brandon Lake and Chandler Moore, Fear is
not my future: song session (YouTube)

Let Him turn it in your favor
Watch Him work it for your good
Cause He's not done with what
He started He's not done until it's good
Hello peace
Hello joy
Hello love
Hello strength
Hello hope
It's a new horizon
If you're ready for a breakthrough
You can open up and just receive
Cause what He's pouring out, is nothing like you've ever seen
The sun is rising, can you see it
Fear is not my future, you are
Sickness is not my story, you are
Heartbreaks not my home, you are
Death is not the end, Jesus you are
Fear is not my future, you are
Sickness is not my story, you are
Heartbreaks not my home, you are
Death is not the end, Jesus you are
Hello peace
Hello joy
Hello love
Hello strength
Hello hope
It's a new horizon, His mercies are new

ABIDE

He defeated death on the cross
He's alpha and omega, the beginning and the end
Goodbye fear
Goodbye guilt
Goodbye shame
Goodbye pain
Goodbye grave
It's a new horizon
Let the light in
It's the morning time, wake up
Joy is coming in the morning time
You don't have to wait on the clock, it's the morning right now
Stop mourning, it's the morning time
Joy is coming
He's risen
Let the light on in.

Remember
Bryan and Katie Torwalt, Remember
(Official lyric Video) (YouTube)

How quickly we forget the God who lives in every day
How easy to lose sight that you reside in the mundane
How quickly we forget the power that's running through our veins
The kind of power that empties graves
And oh, my soul, remember who you're talking to
The only one who death bows to
That's the God who walks with you
And oh, my soul, you know that if He did
it then, He can do it all again
His power can still raise the dead, don't tell me that He's finished yet
Lest we not forget the voice that's holding back the waves
Was once the voice who told the skies to pour them into place
Let us join the endless song of everlasting praise
The only God who empties graves
His power can still raise the dead

JAMIE MARIE OGIAMIEN (LAMPERT)

Don't tell me that He's finished yet
If you broke through the oceans, you can
break through these chains
If your word made the mountains, you can move them all the same
If death fell before you and it's still on its face, then
the power that raised you is about to move again.

Life after Loss

I began to write out my story of grief and faith in 2022, three years after my brother's accident in early 2019. If I remember correctly, it was inspired after telling loved ones about the ways I was comforted and reassured during a time in my life where hope or peace did not make sense. Yet, God did the impossible; He brought hope and peace to my soul. I remember sitting on the couch one night with my sister-in-love Nosa. I was talking about Seth and how god has been working in my grief, and she simply said, "You should write a book about all this." The thought had never crossed my mind before then. Shortly after her visit and our talk, I started to journal some of the many profound moments I experienced during my deepest moments of grief. And then I began to type them out. This led to me exploring book publishing. I wrote out a few "chapters," which still feels funny to say, and my inspiration grew. Just as I was starting to get serious and excited about the process, I became bedridden with my third round of HG.

I mentioned early in the book how I had HG when my brother passed away while pregnant with my second daughter. My husband and I are grateful and excited to welcome our third daughter in December 2023. Unfortunately, my body does not handle early pregnancy well. I become so violently ill that I cannot, even, keep down sips of water for three to four months. I am unable to switch rooms without becoming violently ill. I can be in a deep sleep with the bedroom door shut, and I will wake up to my husband opening up his toothpaste or deodorant down the hall and become violently ill. My family cannot cook or eat in the house without making me sick. I usually throw up streaks of blood for the three to four months because my esophagus is raw from all the throwing up and dry heaving. About a week into this three-to-four-month period, my doctor has a PICC line placed in order to provide hydration and nutrients, since I am unable to keep anything down orally. So for three to four months, I lay in bed being fed through a line. TV, reading, or looking at my phone makes me sick. I cannot walk without assistance. I only leave my bed to occasionally use the bathroom, which requires help since I'm too weak to walk. Occasionally, I shower with assistance, but that requires a lot of time and energy. I mostly lay on the bathtub floor while my mom or husband bathe me; of course, I throw up the entire time from the smell of the soap or shampoo. I have to wear my hair up the entire time because the smell of my hair makes me sick. We use unscented laundry detergent because that is easier to tolerate than something with a strong scent. I only leave my room to go to the doctors, maybe, once a month. Home health nurses come to me to monitor my labs and TPN (total parenteral nutrition). It always feels like longer than three to four months when all I can do is lay there in agony day after day hoping to feel better the next day.

In July of 2023, I started to feel better and was able to attempt to eat and drink again. It always takes some time to rebuild strength, endurance, and reteach my body to digest food; but, in order, to try to avoid infection or a blood clot, the goal is always to get my central line out as soon as possible. So in mid-July 2023, we removed my central line, and by August 2023, I was able to return to work, as well, as begin writing this story out again.

After sharing my story with family and friends, many had the advice to share more about myself. As well, as, where I am now in my grief, four years after losing my baby brother. They, also, thought it would be beneficial to share more about him as a person.

Who am I? I grew up in a small town, Cloverdale, California. I am the sister of Seth. Daughter of Jim and Cindy Lampert. And now wife of Osagiator, as well as, mother to Olivia, Brooklyn, and now, baby Esther. I loved sports growing up and lived for basketball. I was an avid runner. As a young girl, I was invited to church by my friend and neighbor Andrew. I said no for almost a year before I decided to accept his offer and join him for church. My life was never the same after accepting that invitation. I am thankful for his persistence.

I accepted Christ into my life as an eight-year-old at camp. Life only became harder as I grew into the woman I am today, but I am so very thankful I had/have Christ by my side. He was/is my lifeline.

In third grade, they wanted to hold me back in school. I had a reading and comprehension delay. I did not want to be held back so, instead, my parents sacrificed, in order, to bring me to tutoring two to three times a week. In high school and even college, I carried the insecurities of not being "smart enough" with me. But instead of giving up, I would give it to God. I, literally, prayed over all my school assignments for clarity, understanding, and wisdom. By the grace of God, I graduated toward the top of my class in high school and graduated from a very competitive nursing program at Biola University in 2013. Looking back, I can see the ways God carried me through my studies and graciously answered my prayers for help and understanding. I know I would not be where I am today in my career if it was not for my continued reliance and his abundant grace.

I'm now a RN with a Bachelors degree and a Minor in Biblical studies from Biola University. Currently, I am a night-shift labor and delivery nurse. I started off as an oncology nurse on a step-down unit. As hard as that experience was, I am thankful for what it taught me. From this experience, I grew not only in my assessment skills, time management, prioritization, and ability to handle stressful situation; but also, I learned how to be a presence for patients and family members experiencing their worst days of heartbreak and loss. I can remember moments where God brought me to the bedside to pray over someone as they took their last breath or to hold a family member as they collapsed from grief. I do not see as much tragedy as a labor nurse; it's hard to sustain such a heart wrenching position for life, at least for me. I struggled with severe depression from the regular sadness and had to make a change. I have so much respect and admiration for nurses who choose to step into this field long term. It takes a brave and compassionate soul. While I did not feel I could sustain myself in that area of nursing, I very much feel called and used in the position I am in now. I love what a classmate said at our nursing graduation, "Where God calls, God equips." As far as career goes, I can 100 percent attest to this. Without him, I am not capable, but he equips me as I daily rely on him.

Similar to my career, God led me to a man who puts Christ and then me first (despite my poor choices and shortcomings while dating). I am married to a wonderful man. The type of man I prayed for growing up. While there were heartbreaks, dark seasons, and hurtful relationships before him, God redeemed those situations in which the enemy tried to use, to steal, my identity and confidence. He gave me the most patient, loving, humble, and God-fearing man. He knows my past hurts and fully loves and accepts me. He encourages me, prays for me, and brings the good out of me. He challenges me to be my best self daily, yet, is so kind when I am not. He is wise, hardworking, and loves our children with everything he has. While grieving the loss of my one and only baby brother my husband was there for me. He was grieving as well, but he took on the extra load at home. He encouraged me, was patient with me, and reassured me just as my Savior did. He did not judge me when I couldn't function from the grief or spent days/weeks, unable to be the mom I wanted to be for our children. During my three rounds of HG, and my recoveries from my cesarean births, he helped me heal physically and emotionally. When some of our family did not accept our relationship initially, due to cultural barriers, he was loyal and protective over me, even when it meant losing the relationship of loved ones, possibly forever. God knew exactly who I needed by my side in this challenging life.

We're so grateful for our daughters Olivia (six), Brooklyn (four), and Esther, expected in December 2023. They're such joys and full of compassion. They are feisty, spirited, and born leaders. They love the Lord and love their family/friends. Olivia loves the color blue, dislikes dresses, and wants to be a scientist or zoologist when she grows up. She is wise beyond her years and has a mature pallet to match. She loves interesting facts and loves to play soccer. Brooklyn is cuddly and full of personality. She loves the colors yellow and the color "rainbow." She loves dance class and wearing dresses. She wants to be a mom when she grows up. Esther is still a mystery, but I am excited to see God's masterpiece unfold in her life as well.

My husband and I love to coach. I coach the JV girls' basketball team for my old high school with him as my assistant, and he coaches youth soccer with my help. We love to teach our players discipline, respect, work ethic, fundamentals, game strategy, and the importance of never giving up in order to fight through challenges. It brings us so much fulfillment and purpose to pour into young athletes and kids.

Since my brother's passing, I have grown in understanding of God's love. I thought I knew his love before, but when you hit rock bottom and feel all hope is gone, you're forced to seek. In my seeking, I found an even deeper understanding of a gracious and loving God. A God who meets us where we are, but does not leave us there. A God who carries us through the toughest times. A God who brings blessing out of pain and suffering. A God who cares and has a purpose and a plan even in the pain. A God who never stops "chasing" or loving his children. While I still miss my brother every moment of every day, I have a "blessed assurance." All hope is not lost. He picked me up from my rock bottom and carried me to where I am now. Still longing for Seth and our family to be "complete" again. Still grieving. Still desiring to have him in mine and my daughters lives today, but simultaneously at peace that Seth is more than okay, and we will be restored to "complete" again. Grief doesn't go away; it becomes a part of you, but it does change with time. My mom's friend had this realization: "The same Jamie who sat on your couch screaming from the grief and pain of losing her brother is now writing a book to help others in their grief? The one we didn't know how to comfort is taking her pain and choosing to comfort others with it now? Wow." Wow is correct. What a 180, and I cannot take any credit for it. All I can do is point others to my patient, kind, loving, forgiving, all-knowing, always present, humble, life-giving, reassuring, understanding, able, and passionately pursuing God. I am not where I was. I have hope. I have life. I can be the mom I need to be again. I can be the wife, daughter, friend, and nurse that God called me to be again. I can gift others with the reassurance Christ gave me.

JAMIE MARIE OGIAMIEN (LAMPERT)

The Ogiamien family, Osagiator, Jamie, Olivia, and Brooklyn.

Our last Christmas with Seth in December 2018. I was pregnant with Brooklyn in this picture and would become bedridden a couple days after this was taken.

This is also my last picture taken with my brother. He passed on February 5, 2019. I was bedridden the time in between.

My amazing husband Osagiator.

Starting to feel better from HG in July 2023, a couple weeks before removing my PICC line.

JAMIE MARIE OGIAMIEN (LAMPERT)

Olivia and Brooklyn announcing Esther.

The Ogiamiens on our eighth wedding anniversary July 2023. Shortly after this picture, I was able to get my PICC line out, approximately four and a half months pregnant with Esther.

When our family felt complete, one of my favorite family pictures of all times. The Lamperts and the Ogiamiens. Wish I could get another photo with our Ogiamien girls now.

The Lampert family of four…and the Lampert/Ogiamien family of six.

JAMIE MARIE OGIAMIEN (LAMPERT)

Seth and I as children at the beach.

My brother's HS graduation. I drove all day from Southern California after a sleepless week of finals/packing up my dorm for summer in order to make it. So glad I did.

Seth and me.

Seth's letter to me on my twenty-eighth birthday. He took my husband, Olivia, and I out to a fancy dinner. Then asked my husband to split the bill. This was my last birthday to celebrate with him, and it was perfection. I was sick for my twenty-ninth, January 2019, and he passed the following month while I was still bedridden.

JAMIE MARIE OGIAMIEN (LAMPERT)

Seth's twenty-fifth birthday celebration on the left.
Seth's twenty-sixth birthday celebration on the right,
December 2018, our last birthday with him here.

Our wedding day, July 11, 2015. Seth giving us a hug after making
the entire room laugh harder than we knew possible with his speech.

Our big family including the only picture I have with mine and my husband's side of the family together. As well as an image I had made of Seth and my girls by Katelin Jensen (Made By Kate on Etsy).

JAMIE MARIE OGIAMIEN (LAMPERT)

A photo of Seth snowboarding taken by our uncle Chris. Our uncle Chris now uses Seth's snowboard with his picture attached keeping Seth's memory and love for snowboarding/adventure alive.

Seth playing basketball in high school, the same gym my parents, myself, and Seth all played in. The same gym I get to coach in now that my parents also coached in. And the gym we had his service in after his accident.

The last "Hillside" Christmas that felt complete. Some of our "chosen" family celebrating together.

The bronze wolf urn that found my parents.

One of my brother's best friends wore these cufflinks on his wedding day, made by his wife.

Seth and our cousin Mason.

ABIDE

Seth and his dogs Cassie and Lily. Cassie now lives with our parents. Lily lives with the Silvas, our "chosen" family.

Seth and his dog Amber. Amber passed before Seth. I believe they're together now.

JAMIE MARIE OGIAMIEN (LAMPERT)

Some beloved friends. Some of the stories shared in this book come from friends pictured above. Including the picture from our first "family dinner" after his friend was released from jail.

JAMIE MARIE OGIAMIEN (LAMPERT)

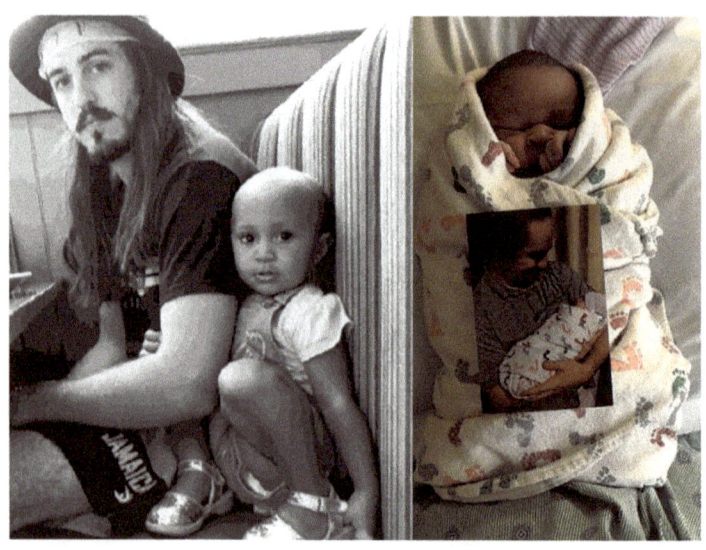

Seth and Olivia, one of my favorite pictures of them. Wishing he could hold Brooklyn as a newborn the way he held Olivia.

Our family with Esther. Shortly after submitting my manuscript where I shared Esther was expected to arrive in December 2023, she decided to come five weeks early. Our December baby is now a November baby and one month old. Wishing I could see my brother hold and love her as well!

ABIDE

Simply Seth. We miss you and love you forever and always.

JAMIE MARIE OGIAMIEN (LAMPERT)

Some of the many photos taken after Seth's accident filled with light and rainbows, usually on special occasions or near things important to Seth.

JAMIE MARIE OGIAMIEN (LAMPERT)

From his service February 2019.

Stories of Seth from the Mouths of Others

Seth as a Person

Seth always made me feel beyond loved. I think of being down emotionally at Thanksgiving one year in Santa Rosa. I didn't get up to hug him as he arrived...I watched him make his rounds with the fam, thrilled to see everyone together! He then sees me on the couch and smiles so *big* saying, "Heyyy, Chels, what's uuuup?" His presence and approach made me feel all in one moment like—I'm here, I got you. You don't have to worry anymore over here in the corner while the rest of the fam doesn't notice how bad off, you're feeling. A sense of "I got you." Just so much love. He came up to me with open arms and hugged me so big and whatever happened after... I don't know, but I was happy because Seth had this type of magical human power. I knew I had someone who had my back no matter what I was feeling or going through. He made me want to keep living that day (Chelsi Long).

*****

When Seth was around six or seven, you, Seth, and I were going to a movie. Seth was upfront, and you were in the back seat. As we were driving along, Seth was sharing with me, so enthusiastically, the glorious nature of the stars and our galaxy. He was just so excited telling me this information. I remember thinking wow this grandchild of mine is so smart and sensitive to this world and so eager to include me with this newfound knowledge. This was unusual, I thought, for a little boy to be so interested in, yet Seth was. You in the back seat weren't that interested in this revelation of his and said so. I loved the beautiful sensitivity of Seth. I loved how eager he was to include people in all parts of his life. Seth was the best friend you could have because he would always have your back, was kind, and always for the underdog. One of my first subbing classes happened to be in Seth's junior high class. One of the students was so unwilling to do the assignment—mind you, his desk was out of sequence to the other desks and purposely right up against the blackboard. First, he said he couldn't do the assignment because he didn't have a pencil then wouldn't take his backpack off his desktop. In my mind, I felt frustrated like this kid was purposefully trying to make my day as hard as possible. I was so upset, I was about to send him to the office, when Seth spoke up and said, "Grandma, he's my friend, and he's having a hard time." I listened to Seth and left the kid alone. Seth had a deep sensitivity to people and was very protective. He was also very, very smart but totally played that down. In another situation, while subbing in his junior high English class, there was a question about the symbolism of a bell in this particular story. I wanted someone to let me know the answer because I didn't have a clue. No one was raising their hand. I looked over at Seth he was sharing something with his desk partner, I asked him what the bell represented in the story, and he knew the answer. I was totally shocked. Things came easily to Seth. He was smart, handsome, compassionate, funny, loving, accepting of others, and a talented athlete. He would put his whole heart and soul into a basketball game, mostly for his team, not a showboat. I miss Seth. I miss so many things about him (Nancy Kemp Davies).

*****

ABIDE

Seth Lampert

A person who had the most life and energy
    to boost
Who always gave a big smile and hug to most

Hillside Drive was where memories were made
From 4th of July to having a kid's parade

Seth won't be forgotten let it be said
From so many who called him our friend

He liked baseball and basketball to name a few
Also compassionate and caring too

Seth was always willing to lend a hand
And always without a great demand

It will be tough day to day
He will be missed by many is for sure to say

From the boy growing up who was always on
    the go
Seth will be with us in spirit as we all know

Not only a family friend but another son to me
He is now in the heavens to finally be free

Seth will be remembered every day
Our thoughts and prayers will never go away

A few words I will miss hearing are "Hey, Big Guy"
But know he is with us up in the sky

JAMIE MARIE OGIAMIEN (LAMPERT)

Seth will be missed by many it is true
But it is a fact WE WILL ALWAYS REMEMBER
AND LOVE YOU!!
(Jay Robinson)

*****

One night, we answered the phone, and it was Seth in a cheery mood, as always. He asked if he could stop by and borrow a hundred bucks. We asked, "Where are you?" He said, "At Willie's" (a seafood restaurant and bar). He then went on to tell us that he was eating dinner alone and met some people at the bar—shocking (not really, haha!). When the bill was brought to him, he realized he got carried away while chatting with his new friends and did not have enough money. He asked the waitress if he could go pick up the money and come right back. How could you say no to Seth? We were cracking up. He could go anywhere and make friends, live in the moment, and not have a care in the world (Christy Russi).

*****

I really need to give honor to this guy, Seth Lampert. I only met him once, but he left a big impression on me. I was stuck and needed a ride, and a friend of mine said he knew someone near there that would be willing to help. So Seth drove an hour out of his way to pick me up. We talked all the way to his house; he cooked me dinner. What I can remember about this night is I felt more love from this guy than I have from anyone else. He deserves honor (Anonymous; this was sent to my mom shortly after Seth's accident from someone we have never met).

*****

On a Poet, Lost

Breath on, breathless poet,
Breath on.
Let the whisper of friends
Be your chest's rise and fall.
Let the life that you've lived
Bring new life to us all.
And so,
Breathe on, breathless poet,
Breathe on.

Write on, silent poet,
Write on.
Let the stories now told
Leave us permanently marked,
And the impressions you've made
Leave our inspirations sparked.
For us,
Write on, silent poet,
Write on.

Move on, restless poet,
Move on.
May your heart keep beating
To the pulse of your song,
The rhythm that you've followed
With which we now sing along.
You must
Move on, restless poet,
Move on.

Live on, absent poet,
Live on.
With every word we speak of you,
In every memory we share,

JAMIE MARIE OGIAMIEN (LAMPERT)

In each act of kindness we pursue,
With each precious thought, you will be there
To leave
Us breathless.
(Austin Schmidt)

*****

I feel I never really talk about Seth because I hate seeing you sad, but I want you to know how much I admired him. He brought an energy and a light very, very few people in this world are able to bring. One memory I have specifically was a Fourth of July party at your house; we were lighting fireworks in the street. I was pretty young, maybe eleven or twelve, but I remember just observing him more than I normally would with a person. And I remember admiring his kindness and love toward other people and telling myself that is the kind of person I want to be. I can still hear his infectious laugh today. When I lost my mom, I thought there was a hole or void that couldn't be filled for the rest my life. It scared me, but as time has gone by, I've come to realize maybe the hole doesn't necessarily need to be filled (Dylan Scaramella).

*****

S is for *San Francisco*, and I was never so grateful for Seth. Sara and Seth were eighteen years old and trying out adulthood. Sara and friends booked a hotel in San Francisco and found an eighteen-and-over dance club. The girls got all dressed up and went. Seth had seen their Facebook post and was also in San Francisco with friends; Seth showed up at the dance club and decided to stay with the girls to make sure they got back to their hotel safely. You might ask why Seth did this. Well, come to find out Seth originally went to have fun with his friends but stayed because he didn't like some of the creeps at the club and wasn't sure these sweet girls were safe. My momma heart is so very grateful because I was a nervous wreck with this being Sara's first trip to the city. But Seth put his plans aside to make sure the girls had a great first trip.

E is for *everyone*. Seth made everyone feel included and important. When Seth talked with me, he had a way of making you feel like you were all that mattered for those few moments.

T is for *tough*. Seth was tough as nails with an adventurous heart. I loved seeing him go through the neighborhood on his motorcycle, bike, car, or skateboard. But he always looked for you to smile and wave. Life was tough on Seth too. Even though he had his own struggles, he always made me feel like I mattered to him.

H is for *hugs*. Seth gave the warmest hugs and no matter who he was with or where you saw him, he would stop and give you that toothy smile and the best hug, that once again, made you feel like you really mattered (Lavon Gambetta).

*****

Any time it was nice outside, the Hillside Crew was out playing in the cul-de-sac. Whether it be a game of kickball, capture the flag, creating forts out of tree branches, or showing off your new toys, we were always outside. I have one vivid memory of Seth that really defines who he was as a person—a jokester. It was a typical day where the Hillside Crew was meeting to play outside for the day. I just so happened to be outside before the rest of the crew and was waiting patiently at the top of the hill for my friends to come strolling up for the day's events. Seth comes riding up on his fancy, brand-new bike and was riding around in circles. What a show-off! He finally asked me if I wanted to take the bike for a spin, and without hesitation, I said yes! Seth had to warn me first that this was not some ordinary bike, no. It was a bike that had a built-in seat that shocked your butt every so often. I didn't want to show my fear (even though I was two years younger than he was) and said that I wasn't afraid of getting my butt shocked. He hopped off the bike and got me ready to go to take this bike for a spin. Around and around, I went with no signs of my butt getting zapped. Just as I thought Seth was full of it, I must have felt something and let out an "Ouch!" I told him I think I felt something and jumped off the bike. We all know that this was not a bike that shocked your butt, but I believed I wanted to be just like Seth: fearless, funny, and well liked. As soon as I looked over, I knew this was all a joke. Seth was crying laughing. I now have a memory that will last forever (Brooke Wenzel).

***

My parents ran into Seth's friend Hopper R. Thomas at a Thai restaurant in town. This was their first time meeting him, in person, though, he has written many kind words about Seth over the years. He hugged my parents and went on to share how he stopped by Seth's old house on the way to the restaurant to ask the new owners if he could have some oranges from Seth's old orange tree that's in the front yard. (My brother's tree had the absolute best oranges, loved by everyone). My dad shared with Hopper how he cloned my brother's tree before they sold Seth's house. Hopper then shared with my parents how he attempted to use the seeds from Seth's oranges to grow his own tree a little while before he passed. He continued to share that shortly before Seth's accident, he told Seth the seeds did not take and they had not sprouted, so unfortunately, he was going to have to get rid of them. Then he heard about Seth's accident and passing, so he couldn't throw them out, just yet, like he had planned to do. Hopper told my parents two weeks after Seth's accident that his orange trees sprouted and have been doing well ever since. (Story told to my parents by Hopper R. Thomas in February of 2024).

Seth. This super suave chappy who will have you drooling at hello. A Seth is a handsome, intelligent witty, guy with snuggles that will make you feel as though you're the luckiest girl on the planet—which indeed you are if you have the fortune of being snuggled by a Seth! This cheeky chap will have beguiled you with his cute boyish charm before you can say wahoo. If you have a Seth, treat him as your king as he is the most hilarious, caring, selfless being alive on this planet today and every moment with this ray of sunshine should be cherished. If you have lost a Seth, miss him with all your heart because he is a once in a lifetime. But remember his carefree laugh and billion-dollar smile, and the way his eyes crinkle and light up when he does, and you'll fall in love again and again. Yep, Seths' steal your heart for good. I'm head over heels in love with a Seth who got away... Do you know where I could find a store which sells Seth's laugh in a jar? (Urban Dictionary) (I read this *Urban Dictionary* definition for Seth at his service because I could not believe how accurately and precisely it explained him.)

To my baby brother

This week has brought me more pain and sadness than I thought humanly possible. I feel like a huge part of me went with you. It is hard to breath at times. My heart aches to see you, give you a long hug and make sure you are ok. I pray you didn't have pain. I hope you are experiencing the freedom and sweet love of Jesus. 2 Corinthians 5 says "when we leave these earthly bodies, we will have a house in heaven, an eternal body made for us by God. While we live in these earthly bodies we groan and sigh, but we want to put on our new bodies so that these dying bodies will be swallowed up with life." You were so full of life and joy. I can't even imagine your new body with even more life and joy. There must be a lot of jokes and laughter in heaven right now. I can't wait to see you again—run and hug you. I look forward to eternity with you. Revelations 21:4 says in heaven "He will wipe away every tear from their eyes, and there will be no more death or sorrow or crying or pain. All these things are gone forever." It gives me peace to know you will never feel pain, sorrow or the sadness of death ever again. You carried a lot of other's pain with you. You loved and cared deeper than anyone I know. You knew how to comfort, give great hugs and hope to those without any. I feel so much comfort knowing that while you still love and care deeply and always will look out for others; You no longer suffer from this sometimes cruel and heavy burdened world. We are blessed with two of the most sacrificially and unconditionally loving parents. We have the most supportive and caring grandparents, aunts, uncles, cousins, village and friends. Olivia loved and adored every second with you. She still talks about Uncle Seth every day and how "Uncle Seth is funny." When I watch videos of you, she jumps up and down clapping, smiling ear to ear screaming Uncle Seth. I think she has your joy—she's been making us laugh during this hard and painful time. She has your ability to see the best in everyone and bring people together. She's been laying on my belly a lot lately while she sleeps. I think her and the baby are already starting to have a bond like ours. Her brother or sister will know everything about their Uncle Seth. I only wish you knew how many people loved and appreciated you. You were such a light in the dark. So many people were impacted by you. Please help me to find some peace in not being able to see you every day or getting to grow old with my brother. Help me not to focus on what we no longer get to experience together, but focus on the many beautiful days we had together. Help me to love and accept others without hesitation the way you did. Help me to lighten up and not stress over the things I'm learning really don't matter in the end. What is important is people. Loving others, cherishing moments, holding loved ones tight and caring for anyone and everyone around you with a need. Nothing else matters. Only love, people and relationships. Help me to be better. Life will never be the same for me here. But help me to give freely and love without fear or hesitation until I receive my new body and meet you in heaven. I love you Seth David-Owen Lampert. I miss you terribly. Rest easy-no more struggle for you little brother. (My speech the day of my brother's service February 2019)

    To start, I would like to thank everyone here for coming today. Leaving the hustle and bustle of this crazy world of modern technology to spend a little time with our family.
    To be honest with you, this might be the only place I could pull this off. The Cloverdale High School Gym has always been a safe place for me as a kid growing up. The gym is a place where you could meet friends, forget about your problems and build structure in your life through basketball. This is where Cindy and I raised our family.

JAMIE MARIE OGIAMIEN (LAMPERT)

Over the past few days, I have had a chance to reflect on my son's life. As a father your job is to teach you children the values you believe in as a parent. One of the things we would always tell the kids growing up is "the person with the most friends in life wins!!!" If you look around, you can see that Seth brought this to another level. That brings me to a little story.

A few days ago, Seth came by the house asking to barrow my jumper box for a friend, "barrow" is the key word. I was a little hesitant at first, but I told him where to find it and asked him to return it to where he had found it. Just like every other dad in this room. For most people this wouldn't be a problem. But Seth was a little different than most kids. He would help his friend get their car going, but knowing they could have this problem again, he would keep my jumper box so that he could offer it to them again. Now you know why I was hesitant to lend it to him. This is the third jumper box in 10 years-coincidentally the same amount of years Seth has been driving.

There are many stories of Seth lending a hand. I could go on and on. But as I sit and think—my son was really teaching me!! We always had a rule in the Lampert family, you could never leave the gym until you made your last shot. So, with that being said, you can take Seth's last shot by reaching out.

The message Seth was sending, was to love your friends and family unconditionally and to take time to listen and be there for people in need. Set aside your differences and open your heart. You can do this with the help of Seth's smile.

I know that is something Seth would appreciate from each of you. I can tell you from where I stand today, the little things in life don't matter.

If you value your friends, family and people in need like Seth—this world would be a better place to live in.

We love you Seth,

Dad and mom

(My dad's speech the day of my brother's service February 2019)

The following are some of Seth Lampert's (Lightning Wolf) many poems:

Duality

Angel or a demon
Lover or warrior
Savior at times or world destroyer
Humiliated then elevated my head stays on a swivel
Knowing when to be which person a task that's far from little
I'm looking for myself with every step and conversation
My mother says the gift of mercy is the cause of my frustration
So I'm mutilated and ripped to shreds when I look amongst
    my peers
I like to say I'm scared of nothing but I have all your fears.

Appreciated

Everyone is selfish including myself
I am sure that I'm less
But there's no way to tell
Negative experiences dwell up inside my head
When left ignored and overlooked they nearly left me dead
My mind becomes hell with a blink of the eye
Will I end up in the burning pit or cross the pearl gates in the sky

JAMIE MARIE OGIAMIEN (LAMPERT)

Weak

Energy is gone and my heart is filled with pain
Can't escape the shame too much dirt is on my name
You can scrub it all you want but there is no way to make it clean
When you came up in the life of living off the triple-beam
Chase my dream in high pursuit
But get too high and loose my roots
At one point in my life my feeders dried up and were gone
Until my tap root reached soul and my foundation grew so strong
How do you get along when your body feels weak?
Exercise your mind until you relearn how to think.

Birthday

Birthdays are a time for joy
But the month is June and I miss my boy
It's hard to find genuine people
In the selfish world there's too much evil
I have fallen victim to the norm
You were my only buddy in the eye of the storm
It's crazy now I'm 25 in 20 days you would be too, but you died
I can't help but feel like you were stolen
My throats choked and eyes now swollen.

Humanity

People say I have reached insanity
But the said truth is I lost faith in humanity
Intentions pure yet I'm in a bind
I love to love is that a crime
Trouble head makes me the outlier
Still the supplier despite my desire
Cry myself to sleep again
Then wipe my tears when a friend walks in
All my loved ones see my hurt

When they feel bad it makes it worse
Stomped on like a brutal hate crime
Do I hate humanity of just my mind
Too bad they're one of a kind
Real lovers love all and not just sometimes.

Music

At the time when the music drops
My heart skips a beat and the whole world stops
With so few dear I've become a rare breed
I care too much and would rather see myself bleed
Misery has been a constant reminder your choices create karma and time will find her
So when the song has struck its last note don't weep for the fallen but remember their quotes.

I love that the common theme learned from Seth's example is to not take life too seriously. To enjoy the small moments and to *love* others sacrificially. This is definitely in line with our Creator's great commandment, highlighted in Matthew 22:37–40. We are called to love one another deeply, above all else (1 Peter 4:8).

Letter in Honor of My Brother

In 2019, the year of my brother's accident, I decided to write a letter to our friends and family. I was really struggling and concerned about my brother's heart toward Jesus, his salvation, and if my faith had been bold enough. After all, I never imagined I would only have twenty-six short years with my brother; I thought we still had many more late nights to stay up and have deep discussions of life and faith. As a way to process, cope, and love others around me the best I knew how, I decided to write a letter to over one hundred people. Close family, friends, Seth's friends whom I knew as well as those I have never met, family/friends that we had lost touch with—anyone and everyone that came to mind.

    I wanted to share a little of my testimony and Seth's journey in order to bring hope as well as the books that had been saving me in my grief, reminding me of the hope of eternity. I was so afraid at the time of saying something "wrong" or not biblically correct that I asked friends, family, and my pastor at the time to proofread my letter before sending it out. I received a lot of good tips and edits, but there were a few that I wish I never took. It made the letter less of my own with wording that bothered me. Since then, I learned that no one really has all the answers; it doesn't matter if they are younger, older, in leadership, etc. We're all as my pastor now would say "under construction." And God is able to work in our shortcomings. We all have a lot to learn and need to approach God with a "childlike faith," ready to be lifelong learners. To feel you have arrived is the work of the enemy in my opinion.

    Since writing this letter and with other questions that came up during my grieving process, I learned that God has given me the gift of discernment, and while I have struggled with confidence in the area of academics or theology my whole life, I can trust the all-knowing God to give me wisdom when I ask. And I know now I won't get it all perfect and that's okay. Often, I look back on things I've said as a child or even last month and feel embarrassed. I'm sure when we get to heaven and our eyes are opened more fully, there will be a lot of those moments. I apologize if I say anything "wrong," but at the same time, this is my story, and God's personal work in my life. Life is messy, humans are messy, and I am messy; but God is good, and he can work perfectly through all our shortcomings. I know I won't write this book perfectly just like I did not get my letter perfect. I hope and pray some of what is written will be encouraging and edifying. I have attached the letter I wrote to family and friends in 2019. I do want to apologize for writing "how do you get right with God" in the original letter. Those were not my words, and while I know God is bigger than one sentence, it has bothered me ever since. In my own words, I would write, "How do you receive this free gift? Just come. Come as you are. Believe in your heart and confess with your mouth that Jesus is Lord, and he will begin to transform your heart, mind, and life. He will love you in such a personalized and intentional way that you will blossom and thrive. Beyond your wildest dreams. His love is that good!"

If you're getting this letter from me, it's because you're someone very dear to me and to my brother Seth. I hope a letter is not too impersonal but the idea of praying and waiting for an opportunity to have a 1:1 conversation with everyone we love seemed like it could take years to accomplish. As we have all seen since Seth's passing life is very unpredictable and not one of us is promised tomorrow. I think all my family and friends know I believe in God, heaven, hell, and I have asked Jesus into my life as Lord and Savior. I do not always talk about the details of my faith out of fear of offending others with different beliefs or sounding crazy. But with Seth's passing I have really been evaluating my faith and what the Bible says about how to truly be saved from this dying world and live eternally in heaven. In my grief I turned to prayer with others, honest heartbroken communication with God, and reading the Bible as well as other books on the topic of death and heaven. While praying with others who believe as I do, crying out to God in desperation for comfort/answers, reading what God says about death in the Bible, and turning to books on the topic—God has both strengthened my faith as well as reassured me that Seth knew Jesus and is safe in heaven now. As my faith grew and I really processed these things that are very hard and maybe impossible to comprehend fully while here; I felt a desperate need to share what I believe with those I love most. I understand that some of you have either slightly or completely different beliefs; I also understand some may believe the same things I do, and this letter will only be a reminder and hopefully encouragement in your faith. I want to make it very clear that I love each of you as you are. I am not trying to change you or make you feel like you're inadequate. If you read this letter and think what I write is absurd and does not spark any interest in you feel free to toss it. But because I am taking the time to write this letter out of love, please just read it and see if it's something that encourages you. If what I write is interesting to you, I would love to talk with you, attempt to answer any questions, give personal stories about my faith, and/or pray with you.

I have been a Christian (asked Jesus into my life) since I was 8 years old. I have had tangible experiences of God working in my life many times through answered prayer, perspective change, spiritual growth, divine intervention, small/large miracles, visions, healing personally/witnessed others being healed, prophesies, and audible words from God. I could write a book on day-to-day tangible experiences with God. Since this letter is already long enough, I will give a quick example of each but if you're interested, I will take as much time as needed to share more detailed examples from each of these scenarios with those of you who want to know.

- Answered Prayer: I could probably give you an example of answered prayer from each day of my life. God is so faithful and good. But one example of answered prayer is God helping me to forgive when I did not think humanly possible. And God's forgiveness in my life although completely undeserved. God has also reconciled very important relationships in my life when I didn't think possible but continued to pray eagerly.
- Perspective Change: Again, there are too many examples I could go on and on. Pretty much every time I pray my perspective on life's situations changes. But the most recent and first example that comes to mind is perspective change in my current grief. I have always believed in eternity after life here but when looking for comfort while missing my brother not only has my faith in heaven increased—But my perspective is much more centered on eternity. The things I use to think were important or major stressors no longer seem that important or that stressful. Life is too short to live in fear. This eternal perspective allows me to look forward to heaven with Seth and place my hope in God's redeeming power rather than my limited body and time.
- Spiritual Growth: Spiritual growth usually happens during hard times in my life or at least that's when I have the most profound spiritual growth. After getting out of a long and toxic relationship I felt a debilitating amount of shame. It was in those two years of deep shame that God taught me the depths of his unfailing love and redemptive power. When I went through a year of depression (after college

while working with oncology patients) I learned firsthand how close God is to the broken hearted and his power to set one free from bondage. And now being the most heartbroken I've ever been my hope in heaven has increased. I have an eternal perspective rather than temporary perspective now more than ever.

- Divine Intervention: When starting to date a guy 10 years ago I pulled up to our first date… when I turned off the car, I heard an audible "NO" and had a strong sense God was trying to protect me or warn me this relationship was a bad choice. I did not listen, and I learned very hard lessons in the 10 months we dated. Ultimately God in his infinite mercy took a bad situation resulting from my lack of obedience and taught me valuable and positive lessons.
- Small/Large Miracles: Many times, throughout nursing school God allowed me to get into full classes that I needed and allowed me to get exact percentages needed to move forward in the program. This was a very competitive program—only thirty-five out of hundreds made it in and anything below a C+ on an exam or for a final grade meant you immediately were released from the program and had to reapply with hundreds of students again the following year. The ways God moved throughout my nursing school experience are indeed miracles and I have Him to thank for being a nurse today. God led me to "random" patients that I was not assigned to and whom I knew nothing about to pray for them as they took their final breath. God also told me to call a friend one day and invite her to church. I thought she would laugh in my face but instead said yes. Months later I found out from her that she was planning to commit suicide that day until she got the call.
- Visions: After a two-year fight with a very close friend, I cried to God in prayer for mutual forgiveness, understanding, and reconciliation. That night I had a dream where I ran into that friend and started up a conversation and we decided to move past our argument. The next day I

ran into my friend in the same setting, and she was wearing the same outfit as my dream. I said what I said in my dream and she responded the same way as well. We are best friends still to this day.

- Healing Personally: When trying to study for a big exam in nursing school I had a three-day migraine that made it hard to think clearly. A Biola student who I had never met came up to me and said God told them to pray over my headache so I could study. He asked if he could lay hands on my head while he prayed and instantly my headache was gone.
- Healing Others: I've seen our church in Southern California come together and pray over a young kid with terminal CA who was healed completely and is CA free to this day. They also prayed over one of our Pastors who was paralyzed in a swimming accident. Medically speaking he was never supposed to walk again but he is a medical miracle. He has run triathlons since his injury and walked to the alter to marry Ehis and I on our wedding day.
- Prophesies: Seth came to Biola to visit me one weekend. He told me about having a near-death experience of his own a few months back. He told me how he saw a glimpse of what he thought was heaven and how confused he had been since. The next day we went to my church Vineyard Anaheim and four or more people who did not know either of us came up to him and said God showed me you in a vision last week. Each person then individually spoke very accurate prophesies over Seth some of which answered the questions he voiced the night before. It was no doubt the Holy Spirit working in them and those words spoken increased both of our faith.
- Audible Words from God: When applying to the nursing program after completing pre-nursing at Biola I was waitlisted. A week and then two went by after the deadline for the waitlist acceptance calls and I had not received any news. Everyone was telling me to start thinking about plan b, but I told them no it's ok God told me I will get in

this year. Sure enough one week later, three weeks after the deadline, I got the call.

I have also seen God love and pursue my brother from a very young age. Shortly after I asked Christ into my life Seth came into my room one night to ask about my faith and ask for prayer. I believe I was about ten years old; I had been walking with Christ for about two years and Seth said he was interested in what I had. After talking through what Seth saw and what Seth wanted, he decided to pray with me. We told God that Seth believed in Him, asked for forgiveness in his life, and asked Jesus to enter his heart and walk with him. I believe, especially after my recent research, from that moment on Seth was saved. I have watched God pursue and love Seth well over the years. I have also seen Seth live out the heart of the Gospel which is love. Seth was full of forgiveness and grace. He always chose to see the best in others. He would give everything he had and then some to anyone in need. He stood up for the weak and falsely accused. He loved the brokenhearted and attempted to comfort those in pain or take on their pain if it meant they would be ok. He never showed judgment or partiality toward anyone. Looking back at his life and hearing stories of his kindness and love has made me realize he was showing me how to be like Jesus more than I was showing him. Seth also had a lot of miracles in his life including a near-death experience in 2013 where he saw glimpses of heaven. I know some of the details to the miracles Seth experienced based on what he told me that I also would be happy to share for those interested.

With Seth's recent passing I have been very comforted in the things he told me about his near-death experience in 2013. I find a lot of peace and hope in the fact that he felt no pain then, and that he was experiencing an overwhelming sense of light peace and love. He told me it was indescribable/hard to comprehend but that it made it hard to wake up every day here having experienced what he did—it had made life seem dull here. At the same time, it stirred up a lot of questions in him and made life more confusing and challenging in some ways. Since it's so difficult to comprehend I can see why it, in a way, made life harder here. Because his experience in 2013 has brought me more comfort than anything I have been consumed with learning more about death, heaven, and what it truly means to be saved. I recently read a book by Dr. Steven W. Long titled Evading Death's Grip. Dr. Steven W. Long is a Christian who had a near-death experience (NDE) and afterwards he was so intrigued by what he experienced and saw that he like me began to dive into the topic except he did his own research I have turned to his and several others. He interviewed 1,500 sources of NDEs and out-of-body experiences including atheist, deaf, blind and as a result has become a well-respected expert in this area of study. I highly recommend the book and if you do not want to buy a copy, you're free to borrow mine just let me know. In his book he recommends the book Imagine Heaven by John Burke also about "NDEs, God's promises, and the exhilarating future that awaits you." I am currently in the process of reading this book and am very much enjoying it so far. The way heaven is described by these hundreds of individuals who have seen it and lived to share brings me so much hope and excitement. It also brings me so much peace to know that Seth is experiencing that now! I have one other book that I plan to read but haven't started yet called Proof of Heaven by Eben Alexander, M.D. who is a neurosurgeon that use to argue that NDEs are impossible, fantasies produced by the brain under extreme stress. After his brain was attacked by a rare illness, he was in a coma for seven days and had an NDE of his own. He could not say his brain produced the "fantasies" he saw because that area of his brain was not working due to his illness. Alexander is now a M.D. and scientist who believes that God and the soul are real, and that death is not the end of personal existence but only a transition. I am very excited to dive into this book more and see a different perspective from someone who was a skeptic and looks at his experiences from a scientific point of view rather than a Christians point of view. Having said that while reading all these books my main source of truth on heaven, death, and salvation is the Bible. I have been struggling with some passages of scripture that seemed contradicting at first read on how to get to heaven; But of course, after a deeper look into the context of what is written I have found these verses are not contradicting at all but just require a deeper understanding. I would be happy to share with you the pieces of scripture that made me ask questions and what I found. And if there is scripture that does the same for you, I would be happy to dive deeper with you in hopes of gaining a better understanding.

Now that I have shared with you where my mind has been regarding death and heaven, I would like to share with you what I believe with my whole heart, and what the Bible states is the way to salvation. Salvation in Christ simply means the ability to walk with Jesus now and live in heaven with Him for eternity after death. But before I share my beliefs and what the Bible says about salvation, I want to share a few things about the life of Jesus, validity of scripture, and character of God:

Life of Jesus

First and foremost, I think it's important to remember that Jesus' life is not only documented in the Bible. There are non-Christian and even anti-Christian sources that state it is a fact that Jesus existed, and was crucified. These same sources state He was believed to be resurrected from the dead and many of His followers were willing to suffer and die for their belief. Prof. Jonathan Morrow, author of "Questioning the Bible" states:

> If Jesus is dead, so is your religion. If Jesus Christ didn't come back to life, it undoes His claim to be the all-powerful, eternal Son of God, Savior and Messiah. So, Christianity hangs on the resurrection. To believe the events around the first Easter, you pretty much have to believe that Jesus did indeed exist and that the New Testament can be trusted. We have far more sources for Jesus of Nazareth than we do for many historical figures in the first century. We have at least eighteen. Twelve of those are non-Christian sources. For some people, they might be ready to believe the Bible is legitimate, but they have a hard time believing Jesus Christ could have actually risen

from the dead. Bible experts say that to dismiss the resurrection, any theory you come up with to explain the historical happenings has to explain away three historical facts: that there was an empty tomb three days after Jesus' body had been placed in it, though it had been constantly guarded by Roman soldiers; Jesus appeared to hundreds of people in numerous places for almost seven weeks after His crucifixion; And something huge did happen to suddenly and forever turn all the cowering, cowardly disciples into bold believers, proclaiming a risen Messiah they were willing to be tortured and died for. Would you die for a lie you made up? Just a few weeks after Jesus' resurrection Peter went from hiding away, fearful the Jewish leaders might have him killed as well, to boldly preaching salvation through Christ before a crowd of thousands, including some of who sought Jesus' death.

Validity of Scripture

As for scripture Prof. Darrell Bock of the Dallas theological seminary explains:

"Any piece of a surviving ancient work is called a manuscript. And more ancient pages or fragments of the Bible have survived by far than any other book from antiquity. Over 5,800 Greek manuscripts and over 8,000 Latin manuscripts. Most books that we work with in the ancient world have maybe at best a dozen manuscripts."

Character of God

Seth and I once went to a church service on God's character at Vineyard Anaheim. Pastor Lance talked about how God's character is multi-faceted like a diamond. Seth loved the analogy he felt like

Pastor Lance wrote his message directly for him—he had an infatuation with diamonds at the time and was very interested to learn more about God after his NDE. God's character is complex and difficult for us to understand at times but also relatable. He is a triune God—Father, Son, and Holy Spirit in one. We are made in God's image and we also have three parts in one—soul, body, and spirit. God is omnipotence—all powerful, omniscience—all knowing, and omnipresence—all present. He is not limited by time or space as we are. God is perfectly loving, holy, and just at the same time. His love is limitless. He created us in His image and created everything good for us. He desires only good for His children (us). He created heaven for humans to enjoy. He desires oneness with us and an intimate relationship like a loving parent with their child. But he gave us the ability to choose freely, we are not His robots. We could force our spouse or friends to act like they love us or begrudgingly live out life with us; But it means so much more when they choose to love us and desire to do life with us. Out of love God gave us the ability to freely choose Him or freely decide not to choose Him. While God is perfectly loving, he is perfectly Holy and Just. He cannot see an injustice and ignore it. There has to be a price for every injustice because He is Holy.

Sometimes as a Christian I think I get too caught up in "doing what is right" now that I have put my faith in Christ and have been saved. But the Bible makes it very clear that Jesus is the way the truth and the life and that no one gets to the father except through Jesus John 14:6. Ultimately this means no one is "good enough" to get to heaven on their own merit. We can never pay the debt fully for our mistakes. I am not trying to insult anyone by saying they are not good enough to get to heaven on their own; this is not a personal jab this is true for all of mankind. This is the reason that God sent his one and only son to die on the cross for the sins of the world John 3:16. (As stated in the previous paragraph: God is a loving God who made human in his image. He wants every single one of us to be saved and live in heaven the way he initially intended; he created heaven for us. But out of his love God allowed us to have personalities and the ability to make our own choices—free will. God allowed free will knowing full well man would make mistakes, we are not perfect, and He knew He would need to make a way for us. God is also just he cannot see an injustice and ignore it. There has to be a consequence for an injustice). God in His infinite wisdom (Omniscience—all knowing) knew man would "fall or sin" make mistakes/not live up to his Holy and perfect standard so He made a way for us. While it is true, we are created in God's image with an innate understanding of good and evil. We are not God and our abilities/understanding are limited. The fact that no one is "good enough" to get to heaven on their own merit is not an insult but a relief. This means that the burden or the striving is off us. It is by grace we have been saved, through faith—and this is not from ourselves, it is a gift from God—not by works, so that no one can boast Ephesians 2:8–9. It is through Christ dying on the cross and taking the sins of the world on his shoulders that we are saved. The consequence has been paid for anything and everything you have ever done with regret. Jesus' act of love on the cross is our free gift, He has removed our sins as far from us as the east is from the west. Psalm 103:12. Colossians 1:22 But now he has reconciled you by Christ's physical body through death to present you holy in his sight, without blemish and free from accusation. Jesus has paid the price for our mistakes however "big or little" they may be. You do not have to change anything about yourself to come to Christ, come as you are. He has given us a free gift of love, acceptance, a clean slate, redemption, new mercies every day, and eternal salvation. All we must do is believe and pray to God with a sincere heart. Tell him you want this salvation. A prayer of Salvation is stating that you believe, asking for forgiveness, and requesting Jesus in your life as Lord and Savior. Asking Jesus into your life as Lord and Savior means there will most likely be some changes in your heart and life as you grow in knowledge and understanding of Him. Jesus as Lord is not a domineering or malicious Lord. He is not a Lord that wants us to end in destruction, Jeremiah 29:11 For I know that plans I have for you, declares the Lord, plans to prosper you and not to harm you plans to give you hope and a future. Jesus as Lord is like a loving Shepard. He will change your heart in some areas and walk closely and protectively in times of distress. He only desires good for His children. He is merciful when we don't always obey in our humanness and limited understanding. Not only does he step in as Lord guiding us out of love, He also steps in Savior. Savior is not only a future promise of eternal salvation but an immediate salvation. Life is hard and bad things happen; it is inevitable. But when you ask Jesus into your life, you're promised his Holy Spirit to come upon you, and the power of the Most High will overshadow you Luke 1:35. Jesus as a Savior meets you where you are (omnipresence—all present) and will never leave you or forsake you Hebrews 13:5. He will be with you through the hills and valleys of life.

A lot of time we look around as if we are in the land of the living waiting to die. When in reality we are in the land of the dying waiting for the land of the living. In Randy Alcorn's book Heaven, he reminds us that the majority of our existence is in eternity (heaven or hell) and only a breath of it is while on this earth. Life here is temporary, it goes by quick Psalm 144:4. But the Bible says if we believe in our hearts and welcome Jesus into our lives, we are guaranteed a house in heaven John 14:2—a new body 1 Corinthians 15:35–58—and an eternity of complete peace without pain sorrow or death Revelations 21:4.

Asking God into your life is very simple. You can ask anytime and anywhere (God is omnipresence—all present). It doesn't have to be fancy. God knows your heart (Omniscience—all knowing). You can whisper it to him now or talk to God privately in your head and He is faithful to meet you where you're at. Simply tell God you believe in Him and accept Jesus as Lord and savior. Ask for His forgiveness and grace over your life. If you believe this, I urge you to pray since tomorrow is not promised. And if you're interested but aren't ready to pray these things, I would communicate that through prayer with God now. Like I said He is faithful to hear you, full of mercy and understanding and loves to meet people where they are at. I have heard so many amazing stories of people going to God with their doubts or questions and Him answering them in many ways.

I believe Seth is in the presence of God and has deep understanding of God love, peace, mercy, light, and goodness right now. We all know when Seth believed something he would go all in and would not withhold any good news from others who needed hope or peace. He would be shouting it from the rooftops. I guess this letter is one way I want to honor my brother's life. He always said he admired how I did not let anyone influence me in the areas I felt strongly about especially regarding my faith. Even though I am still afraid of offending others who do not believe the same as me ... I do not want to keep what I believe to be true with my whole heart a secret. With Seth's passing I realize I may not have tomorrow. So, me sharing what I believe is urgent especially since it has to do with eternity. I want to be open and vulnerable by sharing with the people that both Seth and I love/care for. I hope this letter brings hope rather than frustration. Again, my intentions are not to offend anyone, and I will not be offended if this is not for you. But because I believe these things with my whole heart and it's my source of hope and peace in a very painful time, I felt writing this was one thing I can do out of love and in honor of my brother. Please reach out to me if you have any questions or want to talk.

With love,
Jamie

References

Erik Reed, "Three Keys to Abide in Christ," Open the Bible with Pastor Colin Smith, Subtitle: Jesus Invites you to Abide, April 24, 2017, openthebibile.org.

Bible verses from Biblegateway.com.

Elevation Worship, "Million Little Miracles | Elevation Worship & Maverick City," YouTube Video, 6 minutes 46 seconds, May 10, 2021, YouTube.com.

Elevation Worship, "Give Me Faith | Acoustic | Elevation Worship," YouTube Video, 4 minutes 59 seconds, May 28, 2017, YouTube.com.

Upperroom, "Surrounded (Fight My Battles) - UPPERROOM," YouTube Video, 10 minutes 41 seconds, August 21, 2018, YouTube.com.

Andrew Griggs, "Another In the Fire - Amanda Cook | Bethel Music," YouTube Video, 8 minutes 58 seconds, July 10, 2019, YouTube.com.

Bethel Music, "RATTLE! (Feat. Tasha Cobbs Leonard) - Brandon Lake | House of Miracles," YouTube Video, 7 minutes 18 seconds, August 28, 2020, YouTube.com.

TRIBL, "Jubilee (feat. Naomi Raine & Bryan & Katie Torwalt) | Maverick City Music | TRIBL," YouTube Video, 8 minutes 51 seconds, February 22, 2021, YouTube.com.

Lydia Walker, "What A Friend We Have In Jesus | Lyric Video| Lydia Walker | Acoustic Hymns with Lyrics," YouTube Video, 3 minutes 24 seconds, December 2, 2022, YouTube.com.

Bryan & Katie Torwalt, "Bryan & Katie Torwalt - Sound Mind (Official Lyric Video)," YouTube Video, 7 minutes 36 seconds, May 19, 2022, YouTube.com.

Evan Craft, "Be Alright - Evan Craft, Danny Gokey, Redimiz," YouTube Video, 4 minutes 41 seconds, September 11, 2022, YouTube.com.

Voice Builders, "Good, Good Father (Cover) - Dianne Michelle," YouTube Video, 3 minutes, September 8, 2015, YouTube.com.

TRIBL, "Worthy Of My Song (Worthy Of It All) (feat. Phil Wickham & Chandler Moore) | Maverick City Music," YouTube Video, 8 minutes 27 seconds, April 8, 2022, YouTube.com.

TRIBL, "The One You Love (feat. Brandon Lake, Dante Bowe & Chandler Moore) | Mav City x Kirk Franklin," YouTube Video, 11 minutes 4 seconds, June 29, 2022, YouTube.com.

Bryan & Katie Torwalt, "Bryan & Katie Torwalt - Wouldn't It Be Like You (Official Live Video)," YouTube Video, 9 minutes 39 seconds, May 19, 2022, YouTube.com.

The Ticas Crew, "Promises - Maverick City Music feat. Joe L Barnes and Naomi Raines | Lyrics | Letra," YouTube Video, 10 minutes 48 seconds, April 16, 2022, YouTube.com.

TRIBL, "Ruins (feat. Joe L Barnes & Nate Moore) | Maverick City Music | TRIBL," YouTube Video, 4 minutes 10 Seconds, February 23, 2021, YouTube.com.

Bryan & Katie Torwalt, "Bryan & Katie Torwalt - Simple Kingdom (with Cody Carnes) (Official Live Video)," YouTube Video, 6 minutes 23 seconds, May 5, 2022, YouTube.com.

Essential Worship, "BRANDON LAKE + CHANDLER MOORE - Fear Is Not My Future: Song Session," YouTube Video, 8 minutes 28 seconds, June 20, 2022, YouTube.com.

Jesus Culture, "Bryan & Katie Torwalt - Remember (Official Lyric Video)," YouTube Video, 5 minutes 12 seconds, September 19, 2019, YouTube.com.

Elevation Worship, "Before and After | Elevation Worship & Maverick City," YouTube Video, 8 minutes 39 seconds, May 27, 2021, YouTube.com

Sean Cook, Evan Craft, Willie Gonzalez, "Be Alright (Radio Edit)," Evan Craft & Danny Gokey Lyrics, AZlyrics.com.

Tony Brown, Pat Barrett, "Good Good Father, Chris Tomlin," Lyrics, January 10, 2024, Musixmatch.com.

John Burke, Don Piper, *Imagine Heaven: NEAR-DEATH-EXPERIENCES, God's Promises, and the Exhilarating Future That Awaits You* (Grand Rapids, Michigan: Baker Books, a division of Baker Publishing Group, 2015).

Mary C. Neal, MD, *To Heaven and Back: A Doctor's Extraordinary Account of Her Death, Heaven, Angels, and Life Again. A True Story* (Water Brook Press, 2012).

Randy Alcorn, *HEAVEN* (Carol Stream, Illinois: Tyndale House Publishers Inc., 2004).

Arthur C. Custance, *Journey Out of Time: A Study of the Interval Between Death and the Resurrection of the Body* (Ontario Canada: Doorway Publications, John Deyell Company, 1981).

Marielle Heller, "A Beautiful Day in the Neighborhood," 1 hour 48 minutes, November 22, 2019.

About the Author

Jamie Ogiamien grew up in a small town in northern California called Cloverdale. She grew up in a family that loved sports. Her parents, Jim and Cindy, dedicated a lot of their time to coaching their children and other kids within the community. At age eight, Jamie gave her life to Christ at a Christian camp that her neighbor Andrew invited her to. At eighteen, Jamie left her small town for Biola University, a private Christian university in Southern California, where she studied nursing. In 2013, she graduated from Biola University with her bachelor of science in nursing (BSN) and a minor in biblical studies. She was the first in her family to go to and graduate from a university. While still living in Southern California she met her husband Osagiator, a first-generation Nigerian American. He graduated from San Jose State in 2012 with a masters in occupational therapy. Shortly after, he moved back to Southern California, they met salsa dancing. They now have three daughters, Olivia, Brooklyn, and Esther. In 2016, while pregnant with their first child, Jamie and her husband moved back to northern California, so they would have the support of family while expecting their first child.

In 2019, Jamie lost her younger brother in a car accident; her world felt torn apart. She was three months pregnant with her second child and very sick from hyperemesis gravidarum. Because her brother Seth did not live out the "typical" Christian life, Jamie spent the first year of her grief in constant worry for her brother's salvation and well-being. Because the worry consumed her, she became desperate for reassurance and answers. Throughout her seeking, she met an even more compassionate and gentle God than she ever imagined possible. As her understanding of God's grace grew, she could not keep it contained. She would share this newfound understanding of how profound God's love is and his desperate desire for all to be saved with just about anyone who would listen. One night, while sharing with her sister-in-love Nosakhare, she was given the idea to share about her new understanding of God and how intimately he works in our pain/suffering in a book. And so the process began. Jamie never felt "smart enough" in academia, coming from a small town, being the first in her family to go to college and struggling throughout school. Jamie never felt "good enough" as a Christian due to not growing up in a Christian home, being teased by the other kids at church, and poor choices she made as an adolescent. But thank goodness, God works perfectly in our weaknesses in order to reveal his glory. Who would have thought? Jamie, not "smart enough" or "good enough," labels given to her not from God, would be writing a book and about God. If you asked eight-year-old Jamie, the answer would be "No way." If you asked eighteen-year-old Jamie, the answer would be "No way." If you asked Jamie a year ago, the answer would be "No way." But God!

Before and After
Elevation Worship and Maverick City (YouTube)

I'm a picture of your faithfulness
A miracle in process
Thank God I would have never guessed, that
you were working in the darkness
This is my before and after
There's a new light in my eyes
Some things the camera can't capture
I was dead now I'm alive
You taught my heart to beat again, when everything felt lifeless
You lifted me up from death
And you gave me back my purpose
This is my before and after, there's a new light in my eyes
From the ashes you make beautiful things
I know 'cause you did it in me
I thought it was over, I thought it was done
But you always have the last word, and the last word is love
I barely recognize myself.

Printed in the USA
CPSIA information can be obtained
at www.ICGtesting.com
LVHW012118261124
797345LV00019B/354